MARSEILLES

FRANCE

PAMPLONA

HUESCA ⑩

SARAGOSSA   LERIDA   BARCELONA

Belchite   ⑮

⑫   ⑯
Gandesa   MORA DE EBRO

Vinaroz   MEDITERRANEAN SEA

TERUEL
③ ⑭

VALENCIA

MAJORCA

ALBACETE

IBIZA

MURCIA

CARTAGENA

SPAIN

THE FOUR NATIONALIST COLUMNS MOVING ON MADRID, July-November, 1936 ❶

REPUBLICAN ☐ and NATIONALIST ▩ SPAIN IN DECEMBER, 1936

MAJOR ENGAGEMENTS OF THE INTERNATIONAL BRIGADES ①

1   The Battle in the University City, November-December, 1936
2   The Battle for the Coruna Road, December 1936-January, 1937
3   Republican Operations at Teruel, December 1936-January, 1937
4   Republican Attack at Lopera, December, 1936
5   Republican Operations in the Sierra Nevada, February, 1937
6   Nationalist Offensive at Jarama, February, 1937
7   Nationalist Guadalajara Offensive and Republican Counter-attack, March, 1937
8   Republican Operations on the Pozoblanco Front, April, 1937
9   Republican Attack at La Granja, May-June, 1937
10 Republican Attack on Huesca, June, 1937
11 Republican Brunete Offensive and Nationalist Counter-offensive, July, 1937
12 Republican Aragon Offensive, August-October, 1937
13 Nationalist Attack, Cuesta de la Reina, October, 1937
14 Republican Offensive at Teruel and Nationalist Counter-offensive, December 1937-February, 1938
15 Nationalist Aragon Breakthrough, April, 1938
16 Republican Ebro Offensive and Nationalist Counter-attack, July-November, 1938

LEGIONS OF BABEL

THE INTERNATIONAL BRIGADES IN THE SPANISH CIVIL WAR

Verle B. Johnston

THE PENNSYLVANIA STATE UNIVERSITY PRESS

University Park and London

946.081
J13

Designed by Marilyn Shobaken

to my sons, Derek and Andy

Preface

THIRTY YEARS HAVE ELAPSED since newspapers the world over were featuring stories of the movement of four insurgent columns on Madrid, of the actions of a "Fifth Column" within the city itself, and of the impending fall of the capital. Had it occurred, and the fall of Madrid seemed but a matter of hours away on November 7, 1936, the Spanish Civil War might well have ended then and there. But Madrid did not capitulate; at the eleventh hour a contingent of some 2,000 men from many lands, speaking, shouting, and singing in many tongues, marched down the Gran Via and helped stop the advancing rebels at the city gates. The war lasted another twenty-eight months.

A definitive history of the "International" volunteers who fought for the Spanish Republican Government in the 1936-39 Civil War has yet to be written, and the historian who assumes the task will struggle not only with conflicting accounts from the Right and Left, but with those of partisans of the same camp. Apparently few official records regarding the international volunteers were kept at the time, and even those who held positions of the highest responsibility in the International Brigades, and in the Spanish Government itself, did not know the facts. As Salvador de Madariaga recalled (*Spain*—New York, 1943—p. 9), "Information was confused, biased both ways, hardly ever objective. Within one hour and one hundred yards, one could hear in Paris the effectives of the International Brigade put at 70,000 and at 5,000 by men who had both been present when the Brigades had saved Madrid." And many of the Internationals themselves disagree as to whether the brigades actually "saved" Madrid.

Information concerning the Internationals must of course be weighed very carefully. For one thing, politics within Republican Spain were extremely complex, of which there is perhaps no better illustration than the "right-wing" orientation of the Communists within the Popular Front. Relations between Communists, Anarchists, Socialists, and Republicans were considerably less amicable than indicated by the appelation *Frente Popular,* and the defeat of the Republic occasioned some extremely bitter recriminations among the vanquished. Accounts by former government and party officials are often colored by the individual's political affiliation and in many cases clearly reveal a clash of personalities.

Information published during the war also is of limited value since data on names, number, size, and disposition of military units could be of value to the enemy. The fact, too, that the Loyalists were defeated probably has limited the amount of official information, but it may still be of greater value to the historian than at least one brand of official information which different circumstances might have produced, i.e. depending upon which group or groups in the Republican amalgam emerged as the dominant element had the Loyalists been victorious. But while the task of separating fact from fiction is thus more difficult, the story of the International Brigades thereby becomes more intriguing.

The original draft of this book was based largely upon the excellent materials in the Hoover Institution Library at Stanford University and upon information solicited directly from various individuals and organizations in the United States and abroad. It has since benefitted greatly from the comments of Burnett Bolloten, Robert Friedlander, and my wife, Diane, and additional information obtained in Europe, including Spain, incidental to study under the Fulbright program. Finally, the writer would like to extend his particular thanks to John Gates for many valuable comments and criticisms.

V. B. J.

Contents

Maps

LEGIONS OF BABEL

THE INTERNATIONALIST

Ich came nach Spain in Januar
Yo hablar suelement English
But jetz I say, Comment Savar
Wie gehts, Que tal, tovaritsch

Ich faren mit mein ambulance
In woiken shoit and panties
No tengo tiempo por romance
Y arbeit mas duro que antes

Wen abend komt, I say bon soir
Mi convertures alles veloren
Ich bin sehr kalt, but I am told
C'est la guerre, dasder krieg, there's a war on

But underer dings Ich hat gelernt
That mange ist nicht veel
Nosotros fleisch is sometimes burnt
Mit garlis, tambien huile

Pero una idea es uber alle
An idea muy profundo
We'll arbeit schwer for Franco's fall
Und Unidos Hermanos Proletarios en todo el mundo.

The Volunteer for Liberty

1

INTRODUCTION

IN THE MIDDLE of a hot Friday afternoon, July 17, 1936, Colonels Bartomeu, Solans, and Segui, and Commandant Zanon entered military headquarters in Melilla, Spanish Morocco, presented themselves before the commander of the Melilla garrison, General Romerales, and announced that as of that moment a National Movement to liberate Spain from the clutches of Marxism had begun. Protesting his loyalty to the Madrid government, General Romerales was made prisoner by his subordinates and subsequently shot. Colonel Bartomeu officially proclaimed a state of war as troops of the regular army and Tercio de Extranjeros, or Foreign Legion, were ordered from their barracks to take up strategic positions in Melilla. Resistance was completely unorganized and quickly suppressed as government officials, union leaders, and all known Republicans were arrested, among them General Gómez Morato, commander in chief of all Spanish forces in Morocco. Colonel Bartomeu's proclamation was the signal for an insurrection throughout Morocco, and Colonel Saenz de Buruaga seized control of Tetuán with troops of the Foreign Legion as Colonel Yagüe simultaneously effected a rising in Ceuta. It was not until two days later, however, shortly before

17

seven o'clock Sunday morning, that a small monoplane piloted by an Englishman landed at the Tetuán airport with the military governor of the Canary Islands, General Francisco Franco y Bahamonde.

The first news of the rebellion was transmitted by the insurgents over Radio Ceuta; a radio operator at Ciudad Lineal on the Peninsula picked up the broadcast and transmitted the news to Madrid, where the government was taken completely by surprise,[1] rather incredible in view of the civil disturbances, increasing in frequency and intensity, which the country had been experiencing since the elections of the previous February swept the Popular Front into power. The official bliss of the government was not shared by the population at large, however, as rival factions had repeatedly accused one another of organizing and planning a coup d'etat. The Communist *Mundo Obrero,* official mouthpiece of a party which counted but seventeen deputies in the 473-member Cortes (Parliament) and no ministers in the government, bannered a succession of increasingly dramatic headlines in the weeks prior to the military rising. These ranged from a terse "The Masses Must Be Alert!" to a more definitive "In Face of the Known Plans of Reactionary Elements, Enemies of the Republic and People, Solidarity and Support to the Government Are Pledged by the Socialists and Communists."[2]

The latter statement related to the action taken by the Socialist and Communist Parties, various youth organizations, and the Socialist General Union of Laborers (U.G.T.) in formally pledging themselves to defend the government, which at the time was composed entirely of bourgeois Left-Republican and Republican-Union ministers. The action was prompted by the assassination, by "pistoleros" of the Falange, of a lieutenant in the Assault Guards, a body created on the advent of the Republic in 1931. And it was the assassination of this officer which is believed to have provoked the reprisal murder of José Calvo Sotelo, leader of Renovación Española and the most articulate spokesman of the forces in the Cortes arrayed against the Popular Front. Sotelo's death, in turn, allegedly was the spark which set off the insurrection.

News of the rebellion in Morocco was first brought to the streets of Madrid by the press; official announcements from the government were not immediately forthcoming. In fact, bulletins were not released with any frequency until the day following the outbreak of the revolt, when, at 2:45 P.M. (Saturday) the Ministry of the Interior advised the populace that "To guard public opinion against erroneous impressions, it is hereby made known that Radio Ceuta, now in the hands of the insurgents, is passing itself off as Radio Seville and is broadcasting news concerning Madrid and the rest of Spain which is not true. It is a matter of general knowledge that absolute calm prevails everywhere." [3] Designed as it was to reassure an alarmed populace, such a statement was nonetheless absurd. But during the first two days or so of the rebellion, the government knew little more of the true state of affairs than did the man in the street.

The plan of the insurgents was somewhat as follows: General Sanjurjo, leader of an abortive coup against the Republic in 1932, was the nominal leader of the revolt, while General Franco was designated to assume command of the insurrection in Morocco. General Fanjul was to carry out the revolt in Madrid with the forces of the First Division, quartered in various parts of the city. General Goded was assigned the task of directing the revolt of the Fourth Division in Barcelona, while General Mola was to assume command of the Sixth Division with headquarters at Burgos. General Saliquet was to lead the insurrection of the Seventh Division in Valladolid, General Cabanellas was to seize Saragossa with the Fifth Division, and General Queipo de Llano was to secure Seville with the Second Division, stationed in that city, while General González Carrasco was charged with directing the rising of the Third Division in Valencia. But not all of these generals were then in command of the designated units, and in several cases assuming command necessitated the removal of superior officers of strong Republican sympathies. This is one facet of the rebellion which has not always been appreciated by students of the Civil War.

Apparently the rebels originally planned to have the Fifth, Sixth, and Seventh Divisions march on Madrid if the insurrection in the capital failed, but this plan was changed in some respects to one in which the Moroccan units, mainly Tercio and Moors, together with the Second Division in Seville, played the decisive role. Alvarez del Vayo, ex-Foreign Minister of the Republic, claims that "credit must be given to General Franco, who was responsible for the second plan, for his wisdom in deciding that the centre and starting point of the rebellion should be Morocco and not the Peninsula." [4]

The rebels had reason to count upon a fairly short campaign. Certainly the weakness and confusion of the government, which reflected in large measure the suspicion and mistrust among the parties of the Popular Front (to say nothing of the Anarcho-Syndicalists), provided a seemingly logical basis for belief in a quick victory. But far more important, the rebels counted upon the support of approximately seventy-five per cent of the armed forces. Of these, about 117,000 troops, mainly conscripts, were garrisoned in Spain when the war began, and about 40,000 others, chiefly Moors and Legionnaires, were in Morocco. The Tercio, created by King Alfonso XIII in 1920, probably was the most effective force in the army, and at the time of the rebellion consisted of eight reinforced battalions—"Banderas." But despite these factors favoring the rebels, the insurrection did not come off as planned, and its incomplete success set the stage for a war of thirty-two months' duration.

General Sanjurjo, who was living in Portugal at the time of the rebellion, was killed at the very outset in a plane crash. In Seville, on the 18th, General Queipo de Llano, commander of the Carabineros (customs guards), seized command of the Second Division with the aid of two subordinates and imprisoned the division's commanding officer, General Villa-Abraille, a Republican. The army and Falange seized the civil authorities, whose apathy and vacillation were as much responsible for the loss of Seville to the rebels as Queipo's audacity. A reign of terror was instituted against Republicans and the workers' organizations, and the city was quickly secured for the insurgents.

In Burgos, officers leading the revolt on the 18th imprisoned General Batet, commanding officer of the Sixth Division, and with control over the garrison assured, quickly suppressed resistance offered by workers of the Socialist U.G.T. General Batet was shot in February 1937.

In Valladolid, General Saliquet removed General Molero, commander of the Seventh Division, and with the aid of the Falange secured the city for the rebels.

The headquarters of the Eighth Division in La Coruña were seized by rebel officers who overcame the opposition of the division commander, General Salcedo. He too was later shot.

In Saragossa, seat of the War College and General Staff, the Fifth Division under General Cabanellas eliminated strong Anarchist and Socialist resistance, seized the civil governor and administration, and then deployed along the roads to Barcelona and Madrid to forestall the arrival of Loyalist reinforcements. This action of General Cabanellas, and the plan whereby the divisions stationed in the north and south were to move on Madrid, indicates some doubt in the minds of the rebels as to the success of the rising in the capital. And, in fact, the rising of the First, Third, and Fourth Divisions in Madrid, Valencia, and Barcelona were aborted. In addition, refusal by regiments of the Sixth Division stationed in Bilbao and Santander to join the insurgents kept sections of the Asturias and the Basque country in Republican ranks. Similarly, the loyalty of units of the Second Division stationed in Málaga temporarily saved that city and the surrounding countryside for the Republic.

Since the overthrow of the government in Madrid was the goal of the rebels, particular care should have been given to plans for the rising in that city. The same consideration applied to Valencia and certainly to Barcelona, Spain's principal industrial center, citadel of autonomy, and bastion of the industrial proletariat, who swelled the ranks of the Anarcho-Syndicalist National Confederation of Labor (C.N.T.). Nevertheless, the revolt was only halfhearted in Madrid, it never really got under way in Valencia, and though undertaken with some zeal in Barcelona was crushed in wild street battles which culminated in the storming of rebel strongholds—the Atarazanas barracks, the Church of the Carmelites, and the Hotel Colón on the Plaza Cataluñya.[5]

In Madrid, the insurgents counted on army cadets in the Montaña barracks at the western edge of the city not far from the then Presidential (Royal) Palace. In leading the rising, however, General Fanjul did not act with decision, and no effort was made to leave the barracks and seize the civil government or any buildings of strategic value. Partly because of this hesitancy, other elements of the Madrid garrison, including two artillery regiments, refused to join in the insurrection. On the night of July 19, the government began distributing arms to civilians and the various workers' organizations—in response to a general clamor, but against the wishes of President Azaña who feared the consequences of this transfer of ultimate authority to the street. On the following morning, the Montaña barracks were subjected to a mild artillery and aerial bombardment and, following the rejection of a call to surrender, the barracks were stormed by the mob. Unlike most of his associates, General Fanjul was rescued by a contingent of Republican Assault Guards, but only to suffer a belated albeit somewhat more formal execution.

That the failure of the rebels to seize complete control of Spain was due largely to inadequate planning is indicated by the postwar testimony of General Moscardó e Ituarte, military commander of Toledo and director of the School of Gymnastics at the now famous Alcazar. Prior to the insurrection, Moscardó had divided Toledo into sectors and appointed "chiefs" of each sector, with whom he consulted concerning the defense of Toledo "in case there should be a national rising or any provocation by the 'reds'." But on the day the rebellion broke out in Morocco, General Moscardó wasn't even at his post, but rather in Madrid preparing to depart for Berlin to attend the Olympics: "In Madrid I received news of the revolt of the African garrisons, which was the signal expected for the beginning of our Sacred Crusade; so I immediately gave up the whole idea of my journey [!] and returned in haste to Toledo, where I arrived at about three in the afternoon and at once circulated orders to everybody to take up their positions as previously arranged." [6] (The story of the siege and relief of the

23

Alcazar is well known and needs no retelling here.[7]) Perhaps the most damning indictment against the Spanish Republic is that it succumbed to such an ill-planned and mismanaged conspiracy.

As the opposing forces shaped up, the rebels controlled most of the army including the Tercio and the Moors. The conscripts, however, were not too reliable. For their part, the Loyalists could count on about 12,000 Assault Guards[8] and most of the air force. A revolt at the naval base at Cartagena was confined to officers and was quickly crushed by the sailors; the greater part of the small fleet, and naval personnel numbering approximately 18,000, remained loyal to the Republic.[9] But the Republic could count on the services of only some 500 of a total of 15,000 officers of the regular army. And of these, only about 25 had matriculated at the General Staff College at Saragossa. As events in the field were to prove, this paucity of talent placed the Republicans under a considerable, perhaps even a fatal operational handicap. And that even five hundred officers remained loyal may simply have been due to the failure of the rising in the Republican zone. Two of the principal officers in what subsequently became the Republican Army, General Miaja and the then Colonel Rojo, may have successfully eliminated evidence of their membership in the anti-Republican Spanish Military Union.[10]

THE FORMATION OF THE MILITIAS

After its fateful decision to combat the rebellion by distributing arms to the workers, the Ministry of the Interior, on July 20, dispatched instructions to the mayors of all towns in Loyalist hands to cooperate with workers' organizations in forming militia units. It was these units which assumed the task of defending the Republic and which formed the nucleus of what eventually became an army of over 700,000. For six months, however, it was not an army which took to the field but a hodgepodge of volunteers recruited mainly from the street, under Communist, Socialist, and Anarcho-Syndicalist leadership. The great majority of the militias were organized by the various political organizations, directly or indirectly through their labor affiliates, and bore such descriptive appellations as "Youth Guards," "Red Lions," "Iron Column," "October Battalion," "The Pen Battalion," (formed of middle-class office workers), "Lynxes of the Republic," "Durruti Column," and "Pasionaria Battalion." The latter was named in honor of Dolores Ibarruri, member of the Executive Committee of the Communist Party and apparent author of the slogan, "Better to die on our feet than to live on our knees." [11]

An Englishman who was living in Spain when the war began, and who subsequently became an officer in the XV [International] Brigade, has described the manner in which many of the militias were organized: "A group of men belonging to the dominoes club would decide to join the militia, and would choose as their leader the secretary of the club, because he knew everybody, or the best dominoes player because everyone admired his skill. Or the barbers of a suburb of Madrid would join up, and choose one of their number as leader because he . . . possessed a gold medal; the fact that it was a medal for hairdressing did not matter." [12]

Probably the best fighting unit to emerge was the Madrid "5th Regiment" under the command of Enrique Lister, organized by the Communist Party almost immediately after the outbreak of the rebellion. The regiment was formed from various militias which had fought at Alcalá de Henares, Guadalajara, Somosierra, and elsewhere around Madrid in the first few days of the war. A call for volunteers in the July 25 issue of *Mundo Obrero* claimed that the unit, with headquarters in the Salesian convent on the Calle de Francos (!) already counted 8,000 effectives. The cadre apparatus may have been prepared by the Communists prior to the outbreak of the rebellion. The 5th Regiment grew rapidly in spite of very heavy losses and counted about 70,000 effectives on the Madrid front by mid-October.

In accordance with a governmental decree (which the 5th Regiment strongly supported) its personnel were then gradually organized in "mixed brigades," several of which in turn formed the 11th Division, still under the command of Lister.[13] The regiment claimed that 50 per cent of its recruits were farmers and agricultural workers and 10 per cent white collar workers; 50 per cent allegedly belonged to the Communist Party, 25 per cent were Socialists, 15 per cent belonged to "other parties" (presumably Republican, since the Anarchists did not have a "party" as such), and 10 per cent to no party. Eighty per cent allegedly were between the ages of 18 and 25, 15 per cent between 26 and 35, and the remaining 5 per cent were between 36 and 45.[14]

As the first smoke of battle cleared, the war in Catalonia, Aragon, Castile, and the south assumed the character of reciprocal raids into enemy territory, with both sides devoting attention to "cleaning up the rear guard."[15] This was the beginning of the "red terror" in Republican Spain and of the "white terror" in rebel or Nationalist Spain. Each side had its "daybreak brigades" which assumed, sometimes with sometimes without official sanction, the task of eliminating wrong thinkers. The toll was frightful, and after the lapse of thirty years, partisans of one side or the other still may be heard

to argue whether the most heinous crimes were those committed "against Christ" or in his name.

Perhaps more important and fateful for the ultimate outcome of the war than the initial military successes of the
Nationalists, however, were developments during August and
September beyond the Spanish frontier. Without pursuing in
any detail the matter of German and Italian intervention or
the creation of the Nonintervention Committee,[16] we may note
that there is no evidence of German aid to Franco prior to
the rebellion. But on July 22 General Franco sent to Berlin a
German citizen, Johannes Bernhardt, to solicit aid from
Göring and Hitler. Bernhardt was successful, a Spanish
Morocco Transport Company (Hisma, Ltd.) was quickly organized, and as early as August 2 was flying troops from
Morocco to the peninsula.[17] On the same day three Italian
planes landed in French North Africa. The French Government immediately investigated and discovered that the planes,
with military crews and equipment, had landed in the belief
that they were in Spanish Morocco. Papers in possession of
the crews revealed that the planes had been prepared for their
mission as early as July 15.[18]

The tempo of fighting on the peninsula increased during
late August and the position of the Loyalists began to deteriorate rapidly in the face of determined rebel drives on Madrid
from the northwest and southwest. General Mola's northern
army finally stalled in the Guadarrama mountains forty miles
northwest of the capital, but the southern army maintained
the momentum of its advance and took Toledo on September
28, relieving the besieged forces in the shattered Alcazar. On
the following day General Franco officially assumed command
of all the Nationalist forces and proceeded to Toledo in order

to direct the final assault on the capital which lay some fifty miles away over open country with few natural impediments. In the far north the rebels made some progress along the Cantabrian coast and after an extremely bitter struggle took Irun on September 4, In Aragon, Republican militias halted the insurgents along a front running from Huesca south to Saragossa and Teruel, all of which were held by the rebels. The defense of Irun, just across the border from the French town of Hendaye, and the fighting in Aragon appear to have been the first actions in which foreign volunteers fought on behalf of the Loyalists.

THE FIRST INTERNATIONALS

The concept of a crusade against fascism in Spain originated in the West, not in Moscow.[19] The first non-Spanish volunteers were Frenchmen, Italians, Germans, and Poles, many of whom were political refugees and exiles living in France when the war began. By the summer of 1936, Paris had become a principal haven for political exiles and refugees—Socialists, Communist, Anarchist, and Republican—from central and eastern Europe.

A number of foreigners—the present Spanish Government claims the rather unrealistic figure of 15,000—were in Catalonia for a "People's Olympiad" scheduled to commence in Barcelona on July 20.[20] Some of them may well have participated in the street fighting which crushed the rebellion in that city on July 19, and thereafter, singly and in groups, joined the various militias which set off for the front in Aragon. Simultaneously, and without organized recruiting and direction (at least in the beginning), volunteers of every left-of-center political persuasion migrated to Republican Spain from all over Western Europe—and in some cases from certain parts of Eastern Europe as well—slipping over the French border to join the militia columns. The *New York Times* of August 6 reported that Frenchmen were streaming across the border at Perpignan to join the "peoples' militias." A few days later, the Socialist mayor of Cerbere on the French border advised a United Press correspondent that two hundred "specialists" had been directed into Catalonia by a committee headed by himself, and that ten times that many volunteers had been rejected because of the lack of arms and because only technicians were desperately needed.[21] On August 31, the *Times* also reported that twenty-five Belgians had joined the "Popular Front Army" at Irun the day before.

The volunteers collected in units of their own nationality or joined Spanish units of their particular political persuasion. To a considerable extent this was done through militia committees in Barcelona. Such was the case with the French, Germans, and Italians in particular, whose units, called *centuriae* and bearing the names of revolutionary persons, places, and dates, fought in conjunction with the Spanish militias. Fairly typical of these first volunteers was Italian exile Nino Nanetti, a member of the Central Executive Committee of the Italian Young Communist League. He arrived in Barcelona from Toulouse on July 20, joined a Spanish militia on the Tardienta-Huesca front in Aragon, and rose rapidly to the rank of lieutenant colonel. He was later killed while commanding three brigades in the defense of Bilbao in 1937.[22]

Possibly the first entirely non-Spanish unit to be organized was the French Paris Battalion which participated in the defense of Irun.[23] About the same time, however, a number of Poles organized the General Wroblewski Battalion, named for a leader of the abortive Polish insurrection of 1861. Other

29

Poles adopted the name "Dombrowsky," while a number of Hungarians formed a Rakosi group. Italians and a few Swiss fought in Aragon as the Gastone Sozzi Centuria[24] and saw heavy action at Maqueda and Almorox. Other Italians, mostly Anarchists, organized the Guistizia e Libertà [Justice and Liberty] Column under the command of two Republicans, Carlo Rosselli and Mario Angeloni. On August 28 the column went into action with Spanish Anarchist units at Monte Pelayo near Huesca and suffered heavy casualties.[25] This early and seemingly paradoxical solidarity of Italian Anarchists and Republicans, which lasted throughout the war, stemmed largely from their mutual distrust of the Communists.

One of the most remarkable and important of the early volunteer units was the Ernst Thälmann Centuria, named for Germany's leading Communist who was then in a Gestapo prison and was shortly to be executed. Organized by Hans Beimler and the Central Committee of the German Communist Party in exile, the centuria initially counted some eighty effectives, most of whom were Communists living in Barcelona when the war began. In late August it went into action on the Tardienta-Huesca front as an all-German unit. Reinforced in August and September by some three hundred German refugees from France, the centuria grew to a full battalion with an unexcelled reputation before it left Aragon in October to join the first International Brigade forming at Albacete. The English volunteer Wintringham claims that the Germans were used mainly in "very gallant, almost futile repeated attacks on an impossible position," and were a source of wonder to the Spaniards for their "bitter, terrible courage." [26] Recalling the early exploits of the Germans, a Loyalist army publication in 1938 claimed that when the Thälmanns went through their exercises at their barracks in Barcelona, the crowd of onlookers, which included a number of Spanish militiamen, found the sight "a delightful entertainment, which could have no relation to their own problems. . . . They thought it was simply a German way of going on." [27] A few Austrians also fought at Tardienta in August and at Irun in September, most of them exiled Schutzbundlers. Almost a year and a half later they formed their own battalion, the "12th of February," [28] the date commemorating the brief civil war of 1934 between the Austrian Socialists and the Dolfuss government.

There were only a few English volunteers in Spain during the first weeks of the war and probably only a half-dozen or so Americans.[29] But a few English volunteers may have preceded the Germans on the Huesca front in Aragon. John Cornford, a student from Cambridge and a Communist, was known to have been there in August, and a woman volunteer, Felicia Browne, was killed in Aragon on August 25. Apparently she was the first English casualty.[30] Another group of about eight Englishmen organized a machine-gun company at the Sorria barracks in Barcelona early in August and took the name "Tom Mann Centuria." Organization of the unit has been attributed to two east-London garment workers, Sam Masters and Nat Cohen, who were cycling in France at the time of the revolt. One English volunteer claims that the centuria had a pretty good time for itself in Barcelona during its training, after which it applied to join the International unit forming at Albacete in mid-October.[31]

This, then, was the origin and nature of the first movement of volunteers into Republican Spain—a movement reflecting the individual decisions of anti-fascists and a movement which, at the very beginning, was largely unplanned and uncoordinated. But it did not long remain so, as almost overnight

Paris became the headquarters of anti-fascists who were desirous of getting to Spain themselves or of organizing the flow of others who were eager to take up the fight against fascism. The first step in this direction was the establishment, early in August, of a central office in the Maison de Syndicats at 8 Rue Mathurin-Moreau.[32] And the next step was formal contact with representatives of the Spanish Government.

"THE CONCERN OF ALL PROGRESSIVE HUMANITY"

ITALIANS WERE WELL REPRESENTED among the refugees in France and included a number of figures later active in Italian politics. Among these were Palmiro Togliatti, head of the Italian Communist Party until his death in August 1964, who went under the name of "Ercoli" while in exile, and Luigi Longo, Togliatti's successor as party chief, who operated under the alias of "Gallo." Another Communist active in post World War II Italian politics, Mario Nicoletti, assumed the alias of Guiseppe de Vittorio while in Spain. Nicoletti had fled to Switzerland in 1913 with a Socialist comrade, Benito Mussolini, and again went into exile in 1922 when his former colleague rose to power in the vanguard of a different philosophy.[1] The group of Italian exiles in Paris also included Socialist Pietro Nenni, and Randolfo Pacciardi, head of the Italian Republican Party.[2]

Towards the end of August 1936, Longo (Gallo) went to Madrid to discuss with "Medina," "Clavego," and the leaders of the Spanish Communist Party procedures for facilitating the dispatch of Italian volunteers to the Gastone Sozzi Centuria, which was then shifting from Aragon to Madrid at the invitation of the 5th Regiment.[3] At about this same time (the first week of September), Pacciardi also left Paris for Madrid, intending to meet with Longo and Nenni in order to jointly discuss with the Spanish Government (now headed by Socialist Largo Caballero) the formation of an Italian Legion with the Republican forces. Such a legion, which had been suggested to Pacciardi by Carlo Rosselli, would be "independent" of all political parties in the sense of not being under the domination of any one of them, and would be under the command of the Spanish General Staff. It was Pacciardi's desire, however, that the legion be limited exclusively to Italians as an inspiration to their compatriots at home.

Longo introduced Pacciardi to Indalecio Prieto (later Minister of Defense and, as events were to prove, a particular *bête noir* of the Communists) and then took his leave, while Prieto, who was sympathetic to the proposal, took Pacciardi to see Major Estrada, at the moment Chief of Staff of the Republican forces. Estrada was also quite enthusiastic, but Prime Minister Largo Caballero, the ultimate decision maker, was cool to the idea. He apparently insisted that any foreign volunteers be incorporated into existing Spanish units under Spanish officers. Although he subsequently changed his mind, later events were to suggest that his earlier misgivings were not entirely ill conceived. Mainly as the result of his initial decision, however, the formation of an Italian Legion, or any composite International force, was delayed six weeks. In the interim, Pacciardi visited the "Giustizia e Libertà" column in Aragon, and then returned to Paris to await further developments.[4] But the deteriorating military position of the Republicans had already precipitated action in a number of quarters to render assistance to the Madrid government.

As early as July 28 at a meeting in Brussels, the Second [Socialist] International and the International Federation of Trade Unions had adopted a joint resolution promising the Loyalists "every kind of material and moral support." [5] And in Moscow on August 3, a "responsible Soviet official" remarked to Loy Henderson, the U.S. chargé d'affaires, that "if the Soviet Union is to continue to maintain hegemony over the international revolutionary movement it must not hesitate in periods of crisis to assume the leadership of that movement." [6] Until Socialist Largo Caballero became Premier on September 4, the Loyalist Government was composed entirely of bourgeois Republicans, but had Moscow failed to act after this date, such inaction might have affected the Popular Front government in France. Thorez, for example, was apparently very much concerned over the effect upon Communist Party members of any failure to aid the Spanish Popular Front.[7]

Hugh Thomas has suggested another motive for Soviet intervention: to prevent an early Loyalist collapse while mounting an all-out propaganda campaign in Western Europe and thus, if possible, involving France in a war with Italy and Germany—a war in which the Soviet Union could remain on the sidelines.[8] This would certainly have been in line with earlier policy statements of Soviet leaders, e.g., Lenin's speech of November 26, 1920,[9] but a combination of factors probably caused Stalin to intervene.[10]

During the later stages of the war, Italian submarines and Nationalist surface warships prevented Soviet materiel from reaching the Loyalists by sea. In 1936, however, shipments on Soviet vessels from Black Sea ports posed few problems—not even financial problems after most of the Spanish gold reserve reached Odessa on November 6. Soviet equipment may have been in Spain as early as September 8; it had already seen

action by October 24 when Louis Fischer talked to a Ukrainian tank driver at the front.[11] But Stalin found it much more
difficult to provide trained personnel. Even in 1936, and certainly in 1937-38, during the Great Purge, it was impossible
to send more than a few hundred carefully selected Soviet
officers to Spain. Had thousands of "volunteers" been sent,
many of them would have promptly defected. Too, the presence of thousands of Soviet troops in Spain would have given
a handle to Nazi and Fascist propaganda and done more harm
than good.[12] But many unwanted foreign Communists were
available in Russia; a number of them had fought in the Russian Civil War and had later received formal line and staff
training. And the members of the Comintern apparatus abroad
could recruit, process, and dispatch to Spain genuine non-
Soviet volunteers.

Shortly after he arrived in Madrid late in September, Gustav
Regler, the German exile, met *Pravda* correspondent Michael
Kol'tsov, who showed him several telegrams recently received
from Moscow, including one which stated that the Comintern had decided to form an International Brigade.[13] And at
about this same time, Luigi Longo was "commissioned" by
his Spanish associates to accelerate and intensify the despatch
of new volunteers to Spain. He also learned from his Spanish
and French colleagues that all of the organizations in France
which were concerned with helping the Spanish Government
would, under the initiative and direction of the French Communist Party, undertake the recruitment of volunteers on a
"vast scale."

In addition to a headquarters already in operation at the
Maison des Syndicats, the French Communist Party was also
assigned primary responsibility for setting up branch centers

36

to receive volunteers. The French Communist André Marty, together with the Czech Communist Clement Gottwald and (initially at least) Palmiro Togliatti,[14] presided over the organizing committee at the Maison des Syndicats. The committee (perhaps as reorganized) reportedly was under the direction of one Guilio Cerreti (alias "Allard"); almost immediately it established two centers in southern France, one at Marseilles, the other at Perpignan. Recruiting was also stepped up at all of the offices of the Communist Party in France, as well as at those of the trade unions and "democratic" organizations. According to Longo, the first volunteers to respond to the recruiting drive were French and Belgian workers and Polish exiles.

Longo returned to Spain early in October for the purpose of devising some means of facilitating the flow of volunteers from the frontier to the interior. By October 10, some 500 volunteers were at the frontier town of Figueras, an equal number were on the way by boat from Marseilles,[15] and Longo had no idea of what to do with them. In Madrid, José Diaz advised him to meet directly with Prime Minister Largo Caballero and "officially" offer the services of the volunteers to the Spanish Government and also ask for the necessary assistance in getting them organized. Diaz assured Longo that the two Communist ministers in the Government (Jesús Hernández and Vicente Uribe) would do everything possible to secure support for the venture, while Enrique Lister and "Carlos Contreras" warned him of the "hostilities" he would encounter and the "difficulties" he would have to overcome, and provided him with a letter of introduction to their colleagues at the 5th Regiment depot at Albacete. With the first of the volunteers arriving at Albacete on October 12 (followed by Marty and

Togliatti on the 14th), Longo decided that the moment was "opportune" to follow Diaz' advice and "present them officially to the Spanish Government."

With two colleagues, Stephan Wisniewski and Pierre Rebière,[16] he first paid his respects to President Azaña, who received the three-man delegation "cordially" but also briefly and with some reserve. The triumvirate then proceeded to the Prime Minister, with whom they were "more precise," advising him of their desire to place themselves and the volunteers at the disposition of the Spanish Government and General Staff in order to help fight both Spanish and international fascism. Largo Caballero "listened in silence. From time to time he made a sign with his head which was difficult to understand . . . When I [Longo] finished my exposition, another member of the delegation added a little more, but Caballero remained in front of us, stiff, inexpressive, mute." Longo then interjected his plea for help—food, clothing, transportation, and arms—and at this the Prime Minister finally advised the delegation to check with Martínez Barrio, the Republican President of the Cortes. With that, the meeting ended, no doubt to the relief of all concerned, Largo Caballero included.

The Prime Minister, who had previously rejected the proposal for an Italian legion as presented by Pacciardi, appears to have been confronted with a *fait accompli*—an invitation to accept the services of volunteers who already were gathering by the hundreds at Albacete. Longo also adds that he "was not able to conceal" from his comrades and Spanish friends the "strange effect" which Largo Caballero had had on the three-man delegation. Was it simply the temperament of the man? Hostility toward the volunteers? "Suspicious, taciturn," with a "child's vanity," and "politically capricious," he had "collaborated with the military during the Primo dictatorship."

And thus does Longo reveal his hostility towards the man the Communists shortly set out to destroy.

Following their meeting with the Prime Minister, the delegation then saw Martínez Barrio, who had been assigned the task of organizing the first six brigades of the new army and whom they found most cooperative—"an altogether different kind of man." [17] On October 16 or 17, Martínez Barrio, acting with the apparent approval of Largo Caballero, formally ordered a depot established at Albacete for the incoming volunteers.[18]

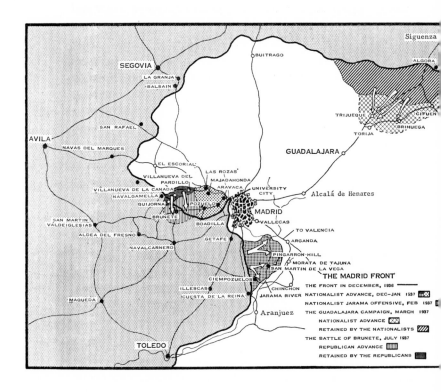

THE MADRID FRONT

THE FRONT IN DECEMBER, 1936 ——————
NATIONALIST ADVANCE, DEC–JAN 1937
NATIONALIST JARAMA OFFENSIVE, FEB 1937
THE GUADALAJARA CAMPAIGN, MARCH 1937
    NATIONALIST ADVANCE
    RETAINED BY THE NATIONALISTS
THE BATTLE OF BRUNETE, JULY 1937
    REPUBLICAN ADVANCE
    RETAINED BY THE REPUBLICANS

3

THE FIRST BRIGADES
AND THE
BATTLE FOR MADRID

IN THE TWO WEEKS after the fall of Toledo, the rebels had advanced to within twenty miles of Madrid. In the open country before the capital, the spirited but untrained and poorly coordinated militias were scattered by the Nationalist aircraft, mostly German and Italian, and were no match for the professional competence of the Legionnaires and Moors.[1] Perhaps the most incredible aspect of the struggle at this juncture was the lack of preparation for defending Madrid itself as the rebels pressed their attack ever closer to the city gates. The absence of trenches and defense lines in front of the city apparently reflected Prime Minister Largo Caballero's belief that Spaniards fought better on rooftops and in trees than in trenches, but even so the front between Madrid and Toledo offered little in the way of rooftops and trees.[2]

Commenting on this phase of the Republicans' "defense strategy," the Madrid correspondent of a London paper expressed astonishment at the Loyalists' "tremendous desire to avoid facing realities. It is fantastic that in these critical moments Madrid should be building houses and an underground railway and laying a new tramcar route downtown." [3] Neither Madrid's construction workers nor the products of its five cement factories were being employed in the construction of trenches, pill boxes, and other defense works. And good crowds still turned out for the Sunday dog races.

On October 28, Largo Caballero put General José Miaja in command of the Madrid garrison, and then, on the night of November 6/7, put him in charge of a Madrid Defense Council composed of representatives of the various political groups. The action was prompted by the now critical military position of the Loyalists. The rebel columns advancing on Madrid from the southwest had reached Getafe by November 5, only eight and one-half miles from the capital. In several places the retreat of the militias degenerated into a complete rout, and the War Ministry was in a state of virtual chaos while political commissars and party functionaries harangued the straggling troops and sent them back to stem the rebel advance. Civilians moving back into the capital before the Nationalist advance added to the confusion by clogging the roads and aggravating the billeting problem.

At midnight on November 5 the government was expanded to include four members of the Anarcho-Syndicalist C.N.T. In entering the government—any government—the Anarchists severely compromised one of their most cherished principles. But the decision to formally participate in the government was made in the belief that the morale of the Anarchist militiamen, who were carrying a goodly part of the fight against the enemy, might benefit from the knowledge that their comrades would have a hand in the decision making process at the highest level. At the same time the Anarchists strongly op-

42

posed a decision of the government majority to evacuate the capital and move to Valencia, arguing that leaders, if at all worthy of the name, belonged behind the barricades with the people they were supposed to represent. Despite these objections, the government moved to Valencia on November 6 and the fate of the capital was left in the hands of the Defense Council.

At 7:00 P.M. on November 6, General Miaja called at the War Ministry and met Generals Pozas and Asensio, the latter then serving as Undersecretary of War. General Asensio gave Miaja and Pozas each an envelope marked "Very confidential. Not to be opened until 6 A.M." General Asensio then left for Valencia, and Miaja insisted that he and Pozas open the letters immediately. On doing so they discovered that the letters had been addressed incorrectly: The instructions in the envelope for General Miaja advised him to proceed to Tarancón to establish headquarters for an "Army of the Center"; the instructions for Pozas were to defend Madrid and to retire to Cuenca in the event that the capital could not be held. It was agreed that their instructions had been mislabeled inadvertently, and the defense of the city remained in Miaja's hands.[4]

The principal problem was arms—many militiamen had to pick them up from fallen comrades. Miaja asked the Central Committee of the Communist Party as well as various trade union leaders for 50,000 volunteers, but when he and his staff tried to determine just how large a supply of arms was available, they were able to locate only 120,000 cartridges by midnight of November 6, six cartridges per each of the 20,000 militiamen believed to be in or about Madrid.

November 6-9 were the crucial days. The rebels moved into

43

the suburbs on November 6 with the capture of Carabanchel Alto after extremely bitter house to house fighting, and had they pressed the attack Madrid might have been taken the same day.[5] The Defense Council, acting on the advice of the Soviet military advisers, ordered the destruction of all bridges as soon as the rebels attempted to cross the Manzanares River into the city proper. The best militia units were deployed at the most critical points, and the 5th Regiment issued do-or-die instructions to the civilian population: "The inhabitants of every block and quarter must organize the struggle at every street crossing, constructing barricades and trenches, forming groups of vigilantes, taking every initiative." [6] Basements and rooftops became miniature fortresses. A "Mixed Fortifications Committee" composed of workers of the Socialist U.G.T. and Anarchist C.N.T. assumed the task of barricading the streets in the western and southern sections of the city. Trees, household furniture, and the street pavement itself were thrown together in the construction of breastworks.

THE FIRST BRIGADES

In the meantime, on arriving at Albacete, André Marty had immediately organized a committee to handle the incoming volunteers.[7] In addition to Longo and Togliatti ("Alfredo"), the committee, which developed into the Political Commissariat of the International Brigades, included Nicoletti, Nenni, and Francesco Scotti, former Secretary of the Communist Party in Milan. In the course of the war the composition of the Commissariat underwent several changes, but always remained under the firm control of Communists.

Nicoletti and Nenni did not arrive on the scene immediately; they were busy in Paris with Pacciardi drawing up an agreement to organize an Italian Legion now that the Spanish Government had modified its earlier position. The agreement, signed by representatives of the Italian Socialist, Communist, and Republican parties on October 27, provided that the Legion would be organized "autonomously," placed at the disposal of the Spanish General Staff, and would serve under Pacciardi. This accord was important in that it placed the direct command of what became one of the best International Brigades in the hands of an ardent democrat, not a Communist. With the signing of the agreement, Pacciardi left for Spain and arrived at Albacete on November 1; he was "greatly surprised" to find the place already swarming with volunteers of many nationalities.[8]

On October 22 the first three battalions of volunteers were formed at Albacete using national groups, and in some cases their earlier battalions, as nuclei. One of these was the predominantly French Commune de Paris created from the earlier Paris Battalion which had fought in Aragon. A second was a German "Hans Battalion" which included a considerable number of Hungarians drawn from the "Rakosi" group. The third was an Italian Battalion, created from remnants of the former "Gastone Sozzi" and "Guistizia e Libertà" units. The three battalions together formed the 9th Mixed Brigade.[9] Volunteers continued to arrive by the hundreds, however, and a fourth battalion was added, the Dombrowsky Battalion composed of Polish and other Slavic volunteers, many of whom had served in the former "Dombrowsky" and "General Wroblewski" groups. At this juncture Pacciardi arrived from Paris and took command of the Italian unit, the name of which was changed to Garibaldi Battalion.

On November 1 the four battalions—the Hans commanded by Hans Kahle, the Commune de Paris under Lt. Colonel

Dumont (with Rebière as Commissar), the Dombrowsky under Tedeusz Oppman, and the Garibaldi under Pacciardi —were formally organized into the 11th Mixed Brigade (replacing the 9th Mixed Brigade), also known as the 11th Mobile Brigade, the First International Brigade and the XI [International] Brigade. Considerable confusion existed, and perhaps still exists, as to the number of International units which fought in the Civil War. Franco himself, in a speech in 1949, referred to "the shock troops of European Communism . . . fifteen international brigades of foreigners, who bore the brunt of the fighting in Spain." [10] But there were only five more or less permanent International Brigades, officially the 11th, 12th, 13th, 14th and 15th Mixed (or Mobile) Brigades of the Republican Army.[11]

The XI Brigade was preparing to leave Albacete on November 4 to help stem the rebel advance on Madrid when word arrived that the German Communist Edgar André had been executed by the Gestapo. As a result, the Hans Battalion changed its name to Edgar André. Then, at the last moment, the Garibaldi Battalion was withdrawn from the XI Brigade to form the nucleus of a second International force. When it finally left Albacete for Vallecas (just east of the capital) on November 5, in response to an urgent appeal from Madrid, the XI Brigade consisted of some 1,900 volunteers.[12]

On the morning of November 6, the Political Commissariat at Albacete received orders to dispatch another brigade to the Madrid front by the following day at the latest. At the time the order came through, only one battalion—the Garibaldi—had been formed, and it had only twenty-five rifles and one machine gun, the supply of arms having been depleted to equip the recently departed XI Brigade. Over half of the volunteers in the camp were still in civilian clothes. It was at

46

this juncture that Louis Fischer arrived on the scene and offered his services to André Marty. Marty promptly appointed
him chief quartermaster, and he thus became the first American to enroll in the International Brigades.[13]

In his capacity as quartermaster, Fischer was responsible
for clothing and feeding the volunteers under conditions of
near chaos. The chief problem was arms; many of the volunteers considered themselves fortunate to receive a rifle marked
"Oviedo, 1896." Many of the weapons were of even more ancient vintage. As many as 3,000 volunteers had to be cared for
at any given time, and the general lack of organization, dearth
of supplies, and overcrowding transformed the depot into a veritable madhouse. On one occasion the commander of one of
the International battalions at the front threatened to send an
armed guard to arrest Fischer for failing to deliver the supplies
which he had demanded. Thus, the arrival of a whole trainload of supplies sent by the French Communist Party was the
occasion for great joy: "As we opened one bale, out came a
baby's rompers," Fischer recalled. "I thought: Those fellows
have gone crazy! Then a silk blouse, then the barrel of a machine gun. They had smuggled through several dozen revolvers too." [14]

Enough men for a second brigade were counted off,
equipped with a hodgepodge of uniforms and arms, and dispatched to Madrid on November 7.[15] This second force, of
some 1,550 men, consisted of three battalions—the dominantly
Italian Garibaldi (commanded by Pacciardi), the basically
German Thälmann (commanded by Ludwig Renn), and the
predominantly French Franco-Belge (also called the André
Marty, commander unknown)—all under the command of
General Lukacz with Luigi Longo as Brigade Commissar. At
this juncture about eighteen Englishmen who had served in

the Tom Mann Centuria joined the machine-gun company of the Thälmann Battalion, inspired by a sign which the Germans had posted on the bulletin board: "We exalt discipline!" This acted as more of an inducement than a sign posted by the French admonishing their volunteers to avoid dens of iniquity.[16]

THE INTERNATIONALS IN MADRID

Late in the evening of November 7 a group of militiamen destroyed a rebel armored car by hurling gasoline-filled bottles (subsequently known as "Molotov cocktails"). On the body of the commander they found some papers detailing General Varela's plans for a final assault on the capital which was to be directed primarily at the area bounded by the University City on the north and the Plaza de España on the south. The militiamen immediately conveyed the papers, marked "General Order of Operations Number 15," to General Miaja and the Loyalist command, which accepted them at face value and redeployed their forces to meet the attack.[17] This came on the morning of November 8, a Sunday, as General Varela, unaware that his plans had fallen into enemy hands, threw some 20,000 troops into an assault along the western and southwestern edge of the capital. "This afternoon we shall have coffee in Madrid," declared Radio Burgos at the seat of the Nationalist high command, and General Mola boasted that with four columns closing on the capital, a fifth column within the city would cut off the Loyalists' retreat.[18] The attack carried forward through the Casa de Campo and just within the Toledo Bridge district a little to the south. A company of barbers hastily formed to meet the attack at the Toledo Bridge succumbed to the last man, and a unit of militiawomen reportedly engaged

48

elements of the Tercio in hand-to-hand combat. An English correspondent observed the fighting in the Toledo Bridge district:

> I saw a sight which made me very ashamed of my petty worries about myself. Going up into the line were long files of civilians. They had no uniforms. Just ordinary suits and a rifle slung anyhow over the shoulder. Most of the rifles were aged and I should say were nearly as unsafe for the man who fired as for the enemy . . . [The defenders] just stayed doggedly in the positions in which they were put and fired their rifles blindly at the foe, when they could see him. The Franco troops too showed great heroism.[19]

The Loyalists did not have nearly enough uniforms to go around, so that frequently a part of a uniform would be allotted to a combatant in the hope of giving him (or her) military status in the event of capture. But this did not always work. On one occasion, a correspondent of the *New York Times* assigned to the rebel forces was on hand when a group of young Loyalist prisoners was brought in. Some of the boys, twelve and sixteen years old, cried; others defiantly shook their fists. Their shirts were removed to ascertain whether their shoulders were bruised from firing a rifle, and those with blue marks were immediately executed.[20]

Another reporter, of the *London News Chronicle*, was drinking coffee at a streetside stand on Madrid's Gran Via on the morning of November 8. Listening to the ever nearer sound of gunfire, his attention was diverted by a commotion down the Gran Via. People began waving their fists and shouting hysterically, "Salud! Salud! Han venido los Rusos!"—"The Russians have come!" The object of their attention, and the cause of the commotion, was a long column of marching men followed by seven lorries and a group of about fifty cavalry.[21] An English volunteer retained a somewhat different impression of the scene: "It was still early, not many people were about. They cheered us and others leaned from windows and shouted. But there was a sense of unhappy apathy everywhere, a feeling of almost hopeless exhaustion . . . Ours was no triumphant entry. . . . and when they saw us and cheered, it was part of the pretence; we were the main actors in the play now, but the illusion didn't work." [22]

The "International Column," as it was first called by the press, passed down the Gran Via to take up positions, the machine gun company of the Edgar André Battalion moving into the University City, the rest of the André and the Commune de Paris moving into the Casa de Campo, and the Dombrowsky joining, for the moment, elements of the 5th Regiment at Villaverde, to the south across the Manzanares. General Emil Kleber, the brigade commander, set up his headquarters in the Faculty of Philosophy and Literature in the University as patrols of the Edgar André established the first contact with the enemy and forced back elements of the Nationalist 4th Regiment.[23]

The XII Brigade, the second of the International Brigades, was not sent directly to Madrid, but, in an apparent effort to divert the rebels from their frontal attack on the capital, was sent south of the city to the vicinity of the Cerro de Los Angeles, a hill which the rebels had secured and from which they were shelling the capital. But the brigade encountered difficulties from the very outset: Transport was lacking, units became separated, and as a result the brigade did not go into action until November 12. In a series of attacks characterized by considerable zeal but even more confusion,[24] the Internationals failed to dislodge the rebels from their vantage point, and were finally withdrawn on or about November 16 and rushed into the line alongside the XI Brigade in the University City.[25]

The arrival of the second contingent of Internationals may have again saved the day, for on the 15th the Nationalists had launched another full-scale attack. Under the cover of heavy bombing, and spearheaded by Moors under Colonel Yagüe, the assault carried across the Manzanares river (on one small bridge) and into the West Park adjoining the Presidential Palace. Though beaten back in this sector by the Edgar André and Dombrowsky Battalions, which were fighting in conjunction with Spanish militia, the rebels penetrated into the University City and eventually reached the School of Philosophy, where they were finally stopped by the Commune de Paris. When it first arrived on the scene, the XII Brigade was put into the line west of the Manzanares between the Hippodrome and the Puerto de Hierro, although the Franco-Belge (Marty) shortly was shifted to support the Commune in the University proper, while the Thälmann relieved the hard-pressed Edgar André in the gardens alongside the Palacete de la Moncloa.[26]

Within the University City, the rebels secured the School of Architecture, the Clinical Hospital (where Moors happily seized rabbits and other culinary delicacies only to discover that they had been inoculated with various germs), the School of Agriculture, and the house of the painter Velazquez, while the Loyalists held the Schools of Science and Philosophy and Medicine. Both sides dug in, and the struggle, which raged for two months almost without a lull, increasingly assumed many of the characteristics of trench fighting during the first World War. In its first month of combat the XI Brigade suffered over 900 fatalities and many more wounded, while the XII Brigade, in its first three weeks of action, had over 700 men killed.[27]

But the rebel losses also were high; one source sympathetic to the Nationalists admitted that the Legionnaires and Moors probably lost as many men in the fighting in and around the University City as they did during the entire advance from Toledo to Madrid: "It was a costly gamble, and one that the Nationalists lost."[28] As demonstrated again in World War II (e.g., Warsaw), a large modern city is a natural fortress. In seeking to take Madrid, the Nationalists were attacking one of the few places the still untrained Republican forces could defend effectively. Had Franco used his best troops elsewhere in open country, perhaps against Catalonia, he might have shortened the war by six months or even a year.

The battle for Madrid as it developed during November and December has been discussed elsewhere.[29] Briefly, however, General Varela, frustrated in his efforts to take the city by a head-on assault, shifted his strategy. On November 29 an attack, led by tanks, was launched to the north in the direction of Humera-Pozuelo-Aravaca-Cuesta de los Perdices with the objective of severing Madrid's communications (and its water and power supply) with the Sierra de Guadarrama. The offensive came to a halt short of Pozuelo in the face of fierce resistance in which Russian tanks and the XII Brigade figured prominently. The Garibaldi Battalion did particularly well, and Pacciardi, its commander, earned the warm accolades of General Kleber as well as a promotion to Lt. Colonel.[30] After the fighting subsided on December 3, the Thälmann Battalion was transferred to the XI Brigade, and the Dombrowsky took its place in the XII, partly for linguistic reasons (the Thälmann, like the Edgar André, was predominantly German-speaking) and allegedly for reasons of temperament as well. The Poles were reputed to have a "temperament" similar to that of the Italians in the Garibaldi (and of the French and

Belgians in the Franco-Belge), with whom they had reportedly established a good rapport while fighting along the Manzanares by the University City.[31]

But the lull in the fighting was only temporary, as General Orgaz, who now replaced Varela, renewed the rebel attack on December 13, hurling some 17,000 troops into an assault against Boadilla. The town was taken after extremely bitter fighting, in the course of which the Thälmann suffered very heavy losses.[32] Resistance again stiffened, however, and General Orgaz suspended his offensive on December 20. Nine days later the XII Brigade, now under the command of Pacciardi, was withdrawn, and, with two Spanish brigades, two cavalry squadrons, and a Thälmann Battery, took part in an offensive along the Guadalajara-Sigüenza highway north of Madrid to forestall an expected enemy attack in this sector. The immediate Republican objectives were Mirabueno, which was taken by the Garibaldis, Algora, which was secured by the Franco-Belge, and Almadrones, which was finally taken by the Dombrowsky on January 3 with assistance from the Italians.[33]

But while the Republicans were completing their operations north of Madrid, General Orgaz unleashed another attack, the most powerful yet, along the entire front from the Casa de Campo to just east of Navalgamella. Three brigades of the old 5th Regiment broke under the fury of the onslaught which was finally contained by the Loyalists on January 15 only after they had yielded Pozuelo, Majadahonda, Villanueva del Pardillo, and, at the northernmost point of the perimeter, Las Rozas. In the first day of the fighting the XI Brigade, with some 1,500 men under the command of Hans Kahle, was thrown into the line south of Las Rozas. Subsequently, the Edgar André was temporarily surrounded near Majadahonda and almost wiped out. Even less fortunate was the Thälmann, deployed along the

53

Coruña highway with orders not to retreat an inch, "whatever happens." Following its orders to the letter, the battalion exhausted its ammunition and was overrun and almost destroyed on January 7. The unit counted only thirty-two survivors. The Commune de Paris fared much better, but still lost well over half of its effectives and had only two hundred survivors after helping to contain the enemy at Las Rozas.[34]

Faced with a major catastrophe, General Miaja then recalled the XII Brigade from Mirabueno and the XIV [International] Brigade (see next chapter) from Andújar in the south. Though exhausted from their previous operations, the two brigades were used as shock troops in a general counter-offensive which began on January 12. Pacciardi's troops failed to take Majadahonda, however; the Spanish brigades under Galan and Nanetti were unable to recapture Villanueva del Pardillo; and the XIV Brigade, after briefly penetrating into Las Rozas, was finally forced to withdraw.[35] The "Battle of the Coruña Road" ended on January 15 with the rebels in possession of twenty kilometers of territory over and above what they held at the end of November, but their efforts to sever Madrid's links with the Sierra, and to drive around the northern perimeter of the capital, had failed. The price in casualties on both sides was enormous.

By this time winter weather had set in, and the elements added to the suffering of the troops in the field. Regler recalled the misery of the combatants during the bitterly cold days of December and January:[36]

The soldiers were coughing, were retching in slimy spasms, or gasping hoarsely from weary chests . . . [Others] were lying in a sodden trench, with a rattle in their throats, overheated by alcohol, and unconscious. . . . Hundreds were tortured by pitiless diarrhea. . . . the fog crept farther un-

der their waterlogged blankets, up the sleeves of their uniforms, down to the skin, bitten raw by vermin. In their
coughs could be heard the despair of creatures under
torture. . . .

No rest since the beginning of November. . . . Often poor
commanders. Heavy losses. In addition, adventurers and
drunkards in every company who are not sent back.

But low morale can hardly have been typical of the Internationals, at least morale low enough to interfere with their
combat effectiveness.

As intense and bitter as the struggle was from November to
mid-January, neither side could effect any substantial gain.
The rebels had failed to take Madrid by a head-on assault, but
they maintained their foothold in the University City. Subsequently, two of the major military operations of the war, the
Nationalists' offensive along the Jarama, and the Loyalists'
offensive at Brunete, were designed to break the stalemate.
Neither of these operations succeeded, however, and until the
day the war ended, a section of the front line dividing Republican from Nationalist Spain looped through the shattered re-
mains of what had been, architecturally at least, one of the
most modern universities in Europe.[37]

In mid-January the XI Brigade was taken out of the line
and sent to a rest camp at Murcia in southern Spain to un-
dergo a reorganization, while the XII Brigade went into rest
and reserve at Vallecas. Since it first went into battle on
November 8, the XI Brigade had lost some 1,230 of its original effectives and now counted (according to one estimate) a
total of 600 survivors in its three battalions.[38] Both brigades
received new volunteers, including at least a few Spaniards,[39]
but it was not yet official policy to fill the Internationals with

large numbers of Spanish recruits, since volunteers continued to flow into Spain from abroad—about 600-700 a week during November and early December.

Possibly the greatest single issue concerning the International Brigades—in this case the XI and XII—is whether they "saved" Madrid. The general consensus seems to be that they did, but the opinion is by no means unanimous.[40] Even some Nationalist historians admit that what frustrated the rebels in their efforts to take Madrid was not only the additional few thousand rifles, but the great spirit and enthusiasm of the men who used them.[41] It was this zeal that fired the Spanish militiamen with a renewed determination not only to hang on but to win. Even the Spanish Information Office (Nationalist) has conceded that the Internationals changed the course of the war, "not because of the military value of 1,900 rifles more but because they reanimated the spirit of the militiamen, inspiring them with a renewed will to fight." [42] Finally, General Kleber, commander of the XI Brigade, claimed that "had we not come, I think the Spanish militia would still have resisted at the gates of Madrid. No doubt we set an example, but it was eagerly followed." [43]

THE COMMANDERS IN MADRID

Just who directed the defense of Madrid during the winter of 1936/37 is not clear. Fischer states categorically that General "Goriev" organized the defense of Madrid through Miaja and his chief of staff. But there is good evidence that General Kleber to some extent pre-empted the function of General Miaja even though the latter remained as nominal head of the Defense Council. General Rojo, Miaja's Chief of Staff, claims that Prime Minister Largo Caballero ordered Kleber not to act on the instructions of General Miaja because the Spanish General Staff (in Valencia) had other plans for the use of the Internationals.[44] One Communist claims that General Kleber, the 5th Regiment, and General Miaja together worked out plans for the defense of Madrid, but that Kleber was, in fact, in charge of the operation.[45] There is little reason to doubt, however, that Kleber in turn worked very closely with the Soviet military advisers, and thereby incurred the displeasure and enmity of General Miaja.

In addition, the foreign press in particular was unstinting in its praise of General Kleber, and he apparently suffered few qualms about accepting these accolades. But the national pride of the Spanish Republicans soared with the successful defense of Madrid, and Miaja and the General Staff did not appreciate the spotlight being focused with such intensity upon a foreigner. It seems to have been for this reason that the Political Commissariat of the International Brigades, either on the request or at least with the concurrence of the Spanish Communist Party, removed Kleber from Madrid very suddenly early in January. When he later reappeared as a division commander in the summer and fall it was without any fanfare whatever.

Kleber's real name may have been Stern. According to an article in the Comintern journal *International Press Correspondence* of December 19, 1936 (pp. 1498-99), he had served in the Austro-Hungarian Army in the World War and had been captured by the Russians, after which he joined the Bolsheviks and fought in the Civil War. He then served in China. Krivitsky claims that he knew Kleber personally when both were students at the Frunze Military Academy in Moscow in 1924, and contends that, despite the dramatic part assigned him in Spain, Kleber actually was without any power in "the inside Soviet machine." [46]

General Lukacz (or Luckacs), the commander of the XII Brigade, had a similar background. His real name apparently was Matei Zalka. According to a Communist source, he was born in Hungary in 1896 in the village of Matolche. Like Kleber an officer in the Austro-Hungarian Army in World War I, he was captured by the Russians. Freed by the Bolsheviks, he was then captured by Czechs but escaped. He took up writing and allegedly joined the Internationals as soon as they were organized. Lukacz was killed in March of 1937 near Huesca when a car in which he was riding with Pacciardi was hit by a shell.[47]

As to Miaja himself, views differ sharply. Wintringham speaks of his "sure hands," but Regler says that "Republican propaganda needed a hero to put on a pedestal." Herbert Matthews claims that "from accounts I received afterwards" Miaja drank too much and lost his nerve. "The picture of the loyal, dogged, courageous defender of the Republic . . . was a myth. He was weak, unintelligent, unprincipled, and in that period his courage could seriously be questioned." Even the circumstances surrounding the selection of Miaja are obscure. Lopez Fernandez (Miaja's aide) contends that Largo Caballero in fact picked Miaja to surrender the city. And after the war General Pozas told Burnett Bolloten that Miaja nearly wept with rage at what he regarded as an attempt to sacrifice him to General Franco.[48]

4

THE JARAMA AND GUADALAJARA

WHILE THE XI AND XII BRIGADES were holding the enemy at bay in the Casa de Campo and University City, two additional brigades of volunteers were organized at Albacete, as well as the first of several international artillery batteries. Generally organized along ethnic lines, the batteries included the "Anna Pauker," largely French and Belgian rather than Rumanian, the "Thälmann" (German), "Skoda" (Czech), "Gramsci" (Italian), the "Daller" (believed to be French), and later the "John Brown" (predominantly American). The equipment of the units consisted mainly of 1914-18 German 105-mm. howitzers with "very delicate mechanisms." Not all of the units were organized in November and December. The "Gramsci," for example, was not organized until January, and the "John Brown" only in April. Nor did the units see action immediately due to a lack of shells.[1]

The XIII Brigade was activated on November 11, primarily with Slavic and French volunteers, although a great many nationalities were represented. The German Communist Wilhelm Zaisser ("General Gomez") was its first commander.

The first unit of the new brigade, initially known as the 8th Battalion, consisted of some 700 volunteers, mostly Poles and Germans, but altogether representing twenty-one nations and including several White Russians. The Germans wanted to adopt the name of John Scheer, a Communist recently killed in a Nazi concentration camp, but instead the unit assumed the name "Tschapaiew" (Chapayev) in honor of a Ukrainian Communist. The other two battalions, the predominantly French 10th and 11th, were merged after heavy casualties in their first action and took the name Henri Vuillemin Battalion. A former editor of *L'Humanité*, Vuillemin had died in the February 6, 1934 street disturbance in Paris. Two other units, the 7th and 9th battalions, were also organized at this time, but were disbanded almost immediately to provide replacements for the XI and XII Brigades. A new 9th Battalion was formed in the XIV Brigade, but apparently the 7th never was replaced as such.[2]

The diverse nationalities in units of battalion and even company size posed a very serious communications problem. The first company of the Tschapaiew, for example, consisted of Germans, Swiss, and, later, Czechs and Palestinians, and called itself the "Storm Column." The second company, "Mickiewicz" (after a Polish revolutionary), consisted almost entirely of Poles, but also counted a few Czechs in a "Gottwald" squad. The third company, "The International Company," was the most heterogeneous. The fourth company (the machine-gun unit) consisted primarily of Austrians who later transferred to the XI Brigade. Many if not most of the first volunteers had been living in France and therefore had a lingua franca. In the newer brigades, however, the diverse languages posed a serious problem, especially when orders had to be translated several times during the thick of the fighting. The mixing of nationalities caused less serious trouble as well. In the Tscha-paiew Battalion, for example, the Germans demanded coffee, while others preferred tea, and the French insisted on wine. These difficulties were subsequently resolved, to a considerable extent, by a reorganization of the brigades along national and linguistic lines. But the exigencies of the moment did not permit the volunteers to be organized on a more rational basis at the time, and the heterogeneous mixtures were simply ra-tionalized as a manifestation of proletarian and anti-fascist solidarity.[3]

The XIV Brigade was organized shortly before Christmas, 1936, with four battalions of about 750 men each: the Nine Nation 9th, the 10th (at first called the "Marseillaise"), the 12th, and the 13th. Like the Tschapaiew of the XIII Brigade, the 9th Battalion was an mixture of nationalities with a com-pany of Italians, one of South Slavs, one of Germans, and one of Poles. The 10th consisted primarily of French volunteers and a few Algerians, while both the 12th and 13th were pre-dominantly French. The 12th also included a sizeable group of English and Irish. During November and December about 500 British and Irish volunteers arrived at Albacete, and 145 of these, joined by five survivors of the English groups in the XI and XII Brigades, were organized in the first company of the 12th Battalion.

The Polish General "Walter"—all "skin and bones" accord-ing to Longo—was put in command of the XIV Brigade, while a French Communist, Heuster, was appointed brigade commissar and an Italian, Morandi, was made chief of staff. General "Walter's" real name was Karol Swierczewski. He had studied and later taught at the Frunze Military Academy in the Soviet Union. After commanding the XIV Brigade in Andalusia, he later commanded the Loyalist 35th Division in offensive operations against La Granja in late May, in the Brunete campaign in July, and in Aragon in the fall of 1937.[4]

On February 8 the XV Brigade was formed at Albacete and three of its battalions, the 600-man British, whose volunteers ranged from 16 to 56 years of age, the 800-man Dimitrov and the 800-man "6th of February" were sent into battle before dawn on February 12. Numerically, the British Battalion was designated the 6th and the Dimitrov and "6th of February" very likely the 14th and 15th. This would be consistent with the numbering of the international battalions up to this time. The appellation "6th of February" commemorated the civil disturbances in Paris provoked by Rightists on February 6, 1934. The Dimitrov Battalion, composed primarily of Slavic volunteers, was named for the Secretary of the Comintern, Georgi Dimitrov. The first company consisted of Czechs, a few Russians (apparently Whites), and South Slavs; the second company consisted entirely of Poles, the third of Italians exclusively, and the fourth, the heavy weapons company, mainly of Poles. The first commander of the battalion, one Grebnaroff, was soon succeeded by Carlo Penchienati, a non-Party Italian. Vladimir Čopic, the brigade commander, was born in Croatia in 1891; drafted into the Austro-Hungarian army in 1915, he was captured by the Russians and "worked for the Revolution" from 1917 on. Although elected to the Yugoslav Parliament in 1920, he was sentenced to prison but escaped. He seems to have been a pretty good baritone and "loved to sing."[5]

Of all the volunteers to serve with the Spanish Republic, the Americans, as a group, were among the last to appear on the scene. The first organized contingent of ninety-six men left New York on the S.S. *Normandie* (third class) on December 26, 1936 and arrived in Spain by way of France on the first day of the new year. Proceeding to Albacete via Perpignan, Figueras, and Barcelona, the men were formally enrolled in the International Brigades at 10:00 A.M. on January 6 and immediately were sent into training at Villanueva de la Jara. In the next year and a half about 3,000 Americans, mostly students with seamen ranking second, crossed the Pyrenees from France in the darkness of night or made the trip to Spain by boat from Marseilles. About 1,000 did not come home.[6]

With the possible exception of the British, the Americans as a group were many years younger than the volunteers of the other nationalities, and were more conscious of their nationality. At first they appeared to be a pampered lot and admittedly were "voluble and militant" in their complaints—particularly with respect to the rudimentary sanitary facilities—and incurred the ire of André Marty. Sandor Voros claims that some of the first Americans were treated with out-and-out hostility by the French in particular, and that at Figueras they were quartered in barracks whose floors were covered with excrement. Later, at Villanueva de la Jara, complaints by Americans about the adequacy of the facilities allegedly provoked a threat from Marty to send them home. But as Gates points out, the Americans came from a country with a high standard of living. They could receive packages from home, but German and Italian exiles could not. Indeed the Americans shared their packages with other International volunteers and Spanish soldiers. The British and French also criticized higher American standards and emoluments in World War II. Longo claims that the Americans arrived relatively well equipped and cites their helmets and warm clothing: "The American committee . . . have done their work well." Rolfe says the first group shopped for "camping equipment" in Manhattan before

63

sailing from New York. Eventually they were an important element in what became one of the best brigades in the Loyalist army and apparently enjoyed considerable popularity among the Spanish people.[7]

The Americans finished their training at Villanueva de la Jara, returned to Albacete on February 15, and were formally organized into the Abraham Lincoln Battalion of the XV Brigade; the 428-man battalion included an all Cuban section and an Irish section. Robert Merriman, a former student and instructor of economics at the University of California, was the first battalion commander. Contrary to some assertions, he was not a member of the Communist Party, but was selected as commander because of his relatively extensive military experience—four years of R.O.T.C. in college![8] The convoy transporting the Lincolns to the front stopped in the hills outside the town of Chinchon and the men were issued grease-covered rifles, which they cleaned with their shirt-tails, and five rounds of ammunition each to fire into a hillside. Of the four hundred and some men, only fifty or so had used a weapon before, and none had used firearms during their recent training.[9]

On December 6, the XIII Brigade was about to depart for the Madrid front when the General Staff at Valencia phoned Albacete and announced that a landing of fascists was believed to have taken place somewhere along the coast to the south. The rumors apparently were prompted by a rebel air raid on the Loyalist naval base at Cartagena, but as a precaution the Tschapaiew Battalion was immediately sent to Valencia. Colodny, however, claims that Largo Caballero ordered the XIII Brigade to stand by so as to have "reliable troops" to put down a rumored Catalonian putsch. Colodny asserts that he obtained this information from Republican officials of "unquestioned integrity." On several occasions over the course of the next two weeks, orders to dispatch the other two battalions of the XIII Brigade were received only to be cancelled, much to the annoyance of the volunteers. Finally, on December 19, orders were received and not revoked, and the 10th and the 11th Battalions joined the Tschapaiew in Valencia.[10]

On December 27 the brigade was moved into action at Alfambra, some twenty kilometers from Teruel, northwest of Valencia and east of Madrid. Seized by the Nationalists at the outset of the rebellion, Teruel was at the apex of a dangerous salient in Republican territory. In a month-long series of attacks—fourteen altogether, several in sub-zero weather—the XIII Brigade unsuccessfully attempted to crack the rebel lines. And casualties were very heavy. The Tschapaiew, commanded by the Swiss Communist Otto Brunner, suffered over 280 dead and wounded while gaining only four kilometers, and the 10th and 11th were so decimated as to require merger into a single battalion, the Henri Vuillemin. Longo asserts that "a single effective command" didn't function during the entire operation, and he mentions poor relations with Spanish Anarchist units which also participated in the attacks.[11]

The XIII Brigade remained on the Teruel front until mid-January, when it was withdrawn and sent to Requena and Utiel in Valencia province for rest and reorganization. Then, following the capture of Málaga by Mussolini's Blackshirts on February 8,[12] the Brigade was sent to Albunol near Motril on February 11. There each of the two remaining battalions was strengthened by some 200 Spanish troops who had participated in the fighting at Málaga (raising the total effectives to about 800 per battalion), and in addition the brigade formally incorporated into its ranks two all-Spanish battalions, the Juan Marco and Otumba. In conjunction with the Spanish 6th Brigade, the XIII on February 19 began a limited offensive high in the Sierra Nevada mountains southeast of Granada. Several villages were taken, including Orgiva (by the Vuillemin), and Pitres, Portuga, and Treveles (by the Tschapaiew), the latter reputed to be the highest inhabited village in all of Spain (over 10,000 feet). The Tschapaiew reportedly took some 800 prisoners in these mountain villages, and their capture may have discouraged any further rebel attempt to cut through the mountains to Almeria on the coast.[13]

Early in April the brigade was shifted to the northwest in the province of Estremadura to meet a rebel attack directed against Pozoblanco and the rich mercury mines at Almadén. The brigade took up positions some forty kilometers northwest of Pozoblanco, and, operating in conjunction with the 6th and 86th Spanish Brigades (the latter contained an international battalion, the 20th—see the next chapter) undertook a series of attacks against Valsequillo (by the Tschapaiew and Juan Marco), La Granjuela, and Blazquez (by the Vuillemin). In hard-fought engagements which commenced on April 4 and lasted through the 7th, and in which the Tschapaiew lost over a quarter of its men on the first day alone, all of the villages were taken by the Republicans. Subsequent efforts to take the rebel-held town of Peñarroya were unavailing, however, and the front then remained fairly stable until the summer of 1938 when the rebels retook the three villages. After that, the front remained virtually unchanged until the closing days of the war.

The XIII Brigade remained on the Pozoblanco front until June under conditions which apparently imposed a severe strain upon morale. In the open, treeless, and scorching plains of Estremadura, the troops suffered severely from a lack of water. Nor were any leaves granted, not even for twenty-four hours, in spite of the promises of the political commissars to "do something." The political commissar of the 20th [International] Battalion, John Gates, states that "almost worse than the action were the long spells of quiet. Periods of inactivity were physically safer, but they also spelled boredom, demoralization." [14]

Meanwhile, the 9th Battalion of the XIV Brigade was dispatched from Albacete to the Cordoba front in Andalusia a few days before Christmas to help contain a rebel advance along the Guadalquivir River near Villa del Rio. In their advance, which was aimed at Andujar and Jaen, the Nationalists employed some six battalions of Moors, together with several cavalry squadrons supported by tanks and planes. In response to a plea from Colonel Sarabia and the 11th Regiment at Jaen (which consisted primarily of C.N.T. militia) the 9th Battalion was first sent to Andujar, and then, on December 24, to Montoro. The battalion, which appears to have been better armed than any of the international units, became lost. No maps were available, and the Spanish commander in the area did not know the enemy dispositions or strength. The companies of the battalion became separated, some crossing the Guadalquivir River only to be trapped behind the rebel "lines." Some 200 survivors (less than a third of the battalion's original strength) lived on uncured olives and herbs and, in small groups, eventually made their way back to Republican territory. [15]

In the meantime, the 10th, 12th, and 13th Battalions arrived from Albacete, and with the support of Spanish brigades under Galan and Carton, launched an attack against rebel-held Lopera on December 27 and 28. In addition, the XIV was supported by the Spanish Domingo Germinal Battalion, a predominantly Anarchist unit which had been organized in November and which was named for a young Spaniard killed in combat at about that time. In the first day of fighting the political commissar of the 12th Battalion, the English writer Ralph Fox, was killed, and the battalion adopted his name as its official designation. The Republican troops were unable to dislodge the enemy, however, and, without any artillery or aerial support of their own, took a fearful pounding from that of the rebels. But they did succeed in halting the drive on Andujar and Jaen, and to this extent their operations might be considered a success.

Accused of treason for the incompetent manner in which he deployed his troops, the commander of the 12th Battalion, Lt. Colonel de la Salle, was courtmartialed and shot. Although Wintringham (p. 89) claims that Commander "L" left his companies in the lurch, Gillain (pp. 31-33) says that de la Salle was shot because of the personal enmity of André Marty. And with the general disorganization and incompetence prevailing in the Republican forces at this time, it is difficult to understand why one unsuccessful officer should have been singled out unless this were indeed the case.

The XIV Brigade remained in Andalusia for only two weeks, and about January 8 was recalled to Madrid, along with the Spanish Domingo Germinal Battalion, to bolster the Loyalist defenses at Las Rozas against General Orgaz' attempt to encircle the capital from the west and north. As we have seen, the attack was halted, but only at the cost of very heavy casualties. In the course of the fighting at Las Rozas, the 13th Battalion adopted the name of Henri Barbusse, the French writer and onetime correspondent for *L'Humanité* who had died in 1935. The 10th Battalion, apparently incorporating a number of Spaniards from the Domingo Germinal, took that unit's name for its own.[16]

At this time too, the surviving British and Irish volunteers in the Ralph Fox [12th] Battalion were withdrawn and returned to the depot at Albacete, where, with a number of recently arrived volunteers, they were organized in an all British-Irish Saklatvala Battalion, named after an Indian Communist. But the appellation never took hold (hardly surprising), and the unit was always referred to as the British Battalion.[17] By the end of January it had a full complement of 600 men, was attached to a newly formed XV Brigade, and rushed to the Jarama River south of Madrid. Frustrated in their efforts to take Madrid by direct assault from the west and by an encircling move to the north, the rebels now attempted an encircling move from the southwest.

THE JARAMA

As the year commenced in January 1937, the fronts in Aragon and Estremadura were both stabilized and relatively calm, a condition imposed mainly by inclement weather. With the exceptions of Madrid and the Asturias, along the northern coast, there was no fighting of any considerable magnitude. The Nationalists were determined to end the war by the capture of Madrid, however, and on January 3, as we have seen, attempted to encircle the capital around its northern reaches from Brunete, Aravaca, Majadahonda and Retamares through El Pardo. This was to be followed by an attack around the southern flank of Madrid to Vallecas and Torrejón. But against the Loyalist resistance in the north, the Nationalists lost fifty per cent of their attacking force, and, as a result, were

69

forced to delay the planned offensive around the southern flank of the capital.

In the meantime, the Republican General Staff had conceived an offensive of its own to be launched from west of the Jarama River just south of the capital. The attack—"a fantastic scheme" according to Colodny—was to cut the rebels' communications with Toledo, and thus relieve pressure on the capital. Colonel Casado, then Chief of Operations of the Loyalist General Staff, claims that the only forces available for the offensive were eight brigades which had just completed training and which were not adequately equipped. Casado objected to the attack on these grounds, and also says that rumors were circulating of an impending attack by the rebels themselves. But these rumors allegedly were discounted by the Loyalists' new Chief of Staff, General Cabrera, and plans for an offensive were being formulated when the rebels unleashed a major attack of their own on February 6, The assault, which involved some 30,000 men including reserves, was directed at the Jarama River in three prongs along a twelve-mile front, the immediate objectives being San Martin de la Vega, La Marañosa (hill), Morata de Tajuña, Arganda, and Vaciamadrid, and the severing of the Madrid-Valencia highway. The Loyalists had only three battalions in the sector (all in the 18th Brigade at Ciempozuelos), the front broke, and the rebel offensive carried to the Jarama River and to the heights overlooking Vaciamadrid on February 8.[18]

When the rebel attack commenced, General Pozas, commander of the Loyalist Army of the Center, ordered General Miaja, chief of the Madrid Army Corps, to send reinforcements, but Miaja refused on the grounds that the troops could not be spared. On Casado's recommendation Miaja then relieved Pozas as commander of the Army of the Center, and four brigades were immediately sent from Madrid to the Jarama front.[19] The XI Brigade, consisting now of the Thälmann, Edgar André, and Commune de Paris Battalions, was hurried into the line from Murcia, where it had been resting and undergoing reorganization, while the XII Brigade, consisting of the Garibaldi, Dombrowsky, and André Marty (Franco-Belge) Battalions, was brought down from Vallecas where it had been in reserve. The Dombrowsky was first deployed near the junction of the Jarama with the Manzanares, while the Marty was sent to a sector along the Jarama, and the Garibaldi took up positions between the Jarama and Arganda.

On February 11 Moors crept in under the cover of darkness and knifed the sentinels of the Marty guarding the Pindoque Bridge over the Jarama. After crossing the bridge, Moorish cavalry then set upon the rest of the Marty Battalion, which had exhausted its ammunition. In the ensuing slaughter, the Moors didn't even spare the wounded who were lying in stretchers awaiting evacuation to the rear.[20]

At this juncture the XV and XIV Brigades arrived, raising the number of defenders to about 30,000. Most of the XV was on hand on February 12, and its Dimitrov Battalion went into action at 5:00 A.M. along with the XII Brigade in an attempt to throw back 10,000 rebel troops under Colonel Assensio who had crossed the Jarama the day before. The battle, which now centered in the hilly area between the Jarama and Tajuña Rivers, reached its maximum intensity. Pacciardi, commander of the Garibaldi Battalion, and his political commissar were among the first casualties, Pacciardi receiving a wound in the head. The 600-man British Battalion, deployed on what became known as "suicide hill," went into action at 5:30 A.M., along with the "6th of February" Battalion (both XV Brigade) and by the middle of the afternoon had lost fifty per cent of its original strength. This first action of the new battalion was as bitter as any it was to experience during the entire course of the war.

At one point in the fighting two days later, the battalion gave way under devastating fire, but, stopped and harangued by General Gall, the division commander, it succeeded in retaking the positions it had lost. Captain Frank Ryan of the Irish section of the battalion described the incident: "Stragglers still in retreat down the slopes stopped in amazement, changed direction and ran to join us; men lying exhausted on the roadside jumped up, cheered and joined the ranks . . . I looked back. Beneath the forest of upraised fists, what a strange band! Unshaven, unkempt, bloodstained, grimy. But full of fight again." [21]

The rebels continued to press the attack, however, and with several thousand fresh troops thrown into the fray on the 14th, forced the Loyalists to retreat, although slowly and at a cost to themselves of very heavy casualties. At this juncture the XIV Brigade, consisting of the remnants of the Nine Nation 9th Battalion, together with the Marseillaise (or Germinal), the Ralph Fox, and the Henri Barbusse, was deployed in front of Morata de Tajuña along the highway to San Martin de la Vega, between the XI and XII Brigades. Fifty tanks also arrived and, under the direction of General "Pavlov," spearheaded an attack by the XI Brigade and the Dimitrovs. The counter-attack sent the enemy into retreat, and for once the Loyalist artillery also was effective.[22]

On February 16, the Lincoln Battalion of the XV Brigade moved into reserve near the front and a week later relieved the exhausted 24th Spanish Brigade in the front lines. At 3:00 P.M. the men went "over the top" in their first action, but the attack failed, partly due to a lack of flank support, and the men revealed their lack of training by bunching together. When the order came to retire, the men bolted straight back to their trenches and sustained miraculously few casualties in the process. One soldier, Joe Gordon, later described what happened: "Word had come through to come back. We were amazed, stunned. After all the advance and all the fighting, to get ordered back! Everybody, First and Second Company in one body, they all arose, stood straight up and dashed back to our trenches."[23]

Apparently in response to the urging of Mussolini's troops fighting in the south, the Nationalists now made one last effort to crack the Loyalist defenses. The fighting again increased in intensity, and in some areas bordered on the chaotic. Remnants of the British Battalion were pinned down by Loyalist machine guns firing from their rear. Wintringham crawled back from the front lines and found some Spanish crews blithely firing away. The officer in charge told him he had merely been ordered to "blaze away into the olive trees."[24]

But the Republicans withstood the renewed assault and planned a counter-attack of their own for the 27th to push the rebels back to and, hopefully, across the Jarama River. Apparently developed either by General Gall, commander of the newly-formed Division "B," or by Vladimir Čopic, the Yugoslav commander of the XV Brigade, the plan called for the Lincoln Battalion to follow the 24th Spanish Brigade in an assault on Pingarrón Hill in the opening phase of the counterattack. Zero hour was set for 7:00 A.M., to be preceded by an intense artillery bombardment of the enemy positions, and the assault was to be supported by both tanks and planes.

At 7:00 A.M. the Lincolns opened up with small arms fire, but there was no artillery preparation, no aerial bombardment, and the 24th Brigade did not leave its positions. Merriman contacted field headquarters on a telephone around 9:30 and was ordered (apparently by Čopic, though it may have been General Gall) to carry through the assault with his battalion alone—"at all costs." A two-hour debate ensued, Merriman insisting that to attack alone would mean the massacre of the battalion, but he was overruled and at noon led the battalion over the top; 127 were killed, including the second in command, Douglas Seacord, and over 200 were wounded, including Captain Merriman. The enemy was not dislodged from Pingarrón Hill, and the 145 or so Americans who survived the debacle apparently suffered a considerable loss of morale.

Wintringham is very critical of General Gall, whose orders to press the attack "at all costs" he brands as "the romantic, unreal view of war, boastful, blindly gallant, that makes courage more important than brains." Ernest Hemingway claims that the whole XV Brigade was almost destroyed "in one single, idiotic, stupidly conceived and insanely executed attack in the hills above the Jarama," and that the man who ordered the attack, General Gall, was afterwards shot when he returned to Russia. "He should have been shot at the time. He was a Hungarian and he hated newspapermen. He had good reason to. For conditions on his front were so deplorable that as soon as they became known, he was removed." Herbert Matthews described Gall as "a Hungarian fighting for the Comintern rather than Spain" and claims that he was reluctant to let correspondents visit the Lincolns on the grounds that they would draw the fire of the enemy and possibly contribute to the casualty lists.[25]

The day after the Lincolns' attack, however, February 28th, the rebels finally gave up their attempt to encircle Madrid from the south, and the Jarama front remained fairly quiet for the rest of the war. About 70,000 combatants—roughly 35,000 on each side—had participated in the battle, and casualties were extremely heavy, with the Internationals bearing much of the brunt of the fighting for the Loyalists[26] and the Tercio and Moors for the Nationalists. The rebels admit that the Tercio lost forty per cent of its effectives, and while claiming that the "Reds" suffered three times as many casualties as the Nationalist forces, nonetheless credit the "marxist hordes" with very high morale.[27]

In summary, the outcome might be considered a victory for the Loyalists insofar as they thwarted the rebels' efforts to encircle the capital. The battle ended on February 28, but many Loyalist units, including the XIV and XV Brigades, had to remain in the lines for another month or more, due to the lack of reserves.[28] Yet the smoke at the Jarama had hardly cleared away before the rebels posed yet another threat to Madrid, this time from the northeast in the vicinity of Guadalajara, and on March 9 the XI and XII Brigades were pulled out of the trenches at Jarama and rushed north to meet the new threat.

GUADALAJARA

The Nationalists had opened a surprise attack about fifty miles north of Madrid, down the highway from Algora, toward the capital. They believed that the Loyalists would not be able to quickly shift their forces from the Jarama, but if they did the fighting there would then be renewed with the aim of closing off the capital in a pincers movement from both north and south. Four divisions of Mussolini's "volunteers," recently transferred from Málaga, formed the bulk of the Nationalist forces, and the offensive began at 7:30 on the morning of March 8. Not more than three Loyalist brigades and scattered

75

militia columns were available to meet the onslaught, and the defense collapsed in complete disorder leaving the road to Madrid wide open. As soon as word of the new offensive was received by the Republican General Staff, the XI Brigade under Lt. Colonel "Hans" was rushed to the vicinity of Torija and assigned to Lister's 11th Division. The XII Brigade was attached to the 14th Division of Anarchist Cipriano Mera and deployed south of the 11th Division on both sides of the Torija-Brihuega highway.[29]

On the afternoon of the 10th, the Garibaldi Battalion repulsed an attack by advance guards of the Italian Black Flames Division at the Palacio of Don Luis south of Brihuega, but the mechanized Black Arrows Division, also Italian, smashed Lister's troops head-on after taking Trijueque, and sent the Loyalists reeling back on Torija. The XI bore the brunt of the attack, suffered very heavy casualties, and, along with a Spanish brigade, was on the verge of breaking in complete disorder. Ludwig Renn, political commissar of the XI Brigade, rallied the troops, however, and the enemy attack was halted just short of Torija.

At this juncture several factors combined to benefit the Loyalists. On the 12th, a number of Russian tanks under General "Pavlov" arrived, and inclement weather enveloped the scene of battle. The Nationalists' airfields were inundated, while the Republicans promptly put every available aircraft (about 100 planes) into the fight.

The Loyalists now found themselves in a position to press limited attacks of their own. Lister's 11th Division recaptured Trijueque in the middle of the afternoon of March 13, as the XII Brigade fought a pitched battle with the Blackshirt Division along the Torija-Brihuega highway where the rebel attack had been repulsed three days before. By this time, the Garibaldis were aware that they were fighting men of their own nationality, and over divided counsel an attempt was made to get the Blackshirts to desert. Exhortations, punctuated with frequent playings of the "Internationale," were broadcast through loud speakers, and the Garibaldis were provided with printed leaflets inviting the Italians to come over to the side of The People. Patrols deposited the messages, wrapped around stones, within the enemy lines. Some French political commissars, as well as a number of the volunteers themselves, were opposed to these efforts, however, and on one occasion the mutilated bodies of several Garibaldis were found with the propaganda leaflets stuck in their mouths. On another occasion Blackshirts besieged in the Palacio de Ibarra hung out a white flag in response to a propaganda barrage through a loud speaker, and then opened fire on the Garibaldis who had left their positions to welcome their errant brethren back into the fold. The Palacio was finally taken by storm.[30]

Following the recapture of Trijueque, fighting continued for several days without any major changes in the front, and Italian General Mancini advised his troops that the resistance of the "Reds" was the resistance which precedes a collapse. But on the 18th General Miaja ordered a full-scale offensive. Following a forty-minute artillery barrage, in which the Skoda and Baller Batteries participated, and with strong air and tank support, El Campesino's 46th Division, with the Edgar André and Thälmann Battalions of the XI Brigade, led an assault against Brihuega from the west, as the XII Brigade led an attack from the east. Caught in a pincers, the Italian Blackshirt and Littorio Divisions broke in a complete rout and fled down the highway toward Siguenza. The Republican air force raised havoc with the fleeing Italians, and the XI, XII, and 35th Brigades pressed the attack until, exhausted, they could go no farther.

When the Battle of Guadalajara came to an end on March 23 the Blackshirt Division had virtually ceased to exist as a military unit. Casualties on both sides were very high, but reliable estimates of the losses sustained by Il Duce's legions, including dead, wounded and prisoners, run as high as 12,000. According to *Épopée* (p. 109) the booty included 30 pieces of artillery, 150 machine guns, 1,300 trucks and other vehicles, and thousands of rifles.[31]

The Republicans also captured a number of documents which they published to prove the scope and nature of Italian intervention:

> I am receiving on board the Pola on my way to Libya the communiqués of the great battle in progress in the direction of Guadalajara . . . [Mussolini had wired General Mancini] I am certain that the dash and tenacity of our legionnaires will sweep away the enemy's resistance. The rout of the international forces will be a success of great value, also from the political point of view. Tell the legionnaires that I myself am following hour by hour their movements, which will be crowned with victory.

And in an order to divisional commanders on March 17, General Mancini had advised them to tell the troops "that the International Brigades, although composed of better fighters than the ordinary Spanish militiamen, are few in numbers . . . Moreover, these men are the same as, or brothers so to speak, of those whom our Fascist squads thoroughly thrashed on the roads of Italy." [32]

Although the Loyalists admit that the Nationalist attack

was stupidly directed and executed, they claim that the frustration of the offensive was due primarily to the spirit of the Republican troops, who for the first time really came to grips with the "foreign invaders." [33] Again, as at Madrid and the Jarama, the victory of the Republicans was largely defensive, but it did give a tremendous boost to their morale, and, perhaps more important, demonstrated that they were capable of maneuver and attack as well as purely defensive operations. Colodny (pp. 229-30, n. 161) maintains that it would be incorrect to assert that the Internationals bore the weight of the Guadalajara campaign, since the XI and XII Brigades together probably counted no more than 3,000 effectives. But he does point out that they were shock troops, and at Guadalajara, as at the Jarama and Madrid, the Internationals tipped the balance.

5

SOME ORDER
FROM CHAOS

THE TERMINATION OF THE FIGHTING at Guadalajara in March initiated a three-month interlude of relative calm on the main fronts. Having failed in three major attempts to take Madrid, General Franco directed his energies to eliminating the isolated but politically and industrially important sector held by the Republicans along the Bay of Biscay and the Cantabrian coast. Bilbao was an important producer of steel, the bulk of Spain's coal came from the mines of the Asturias, and the support given the Republicans by the Basque Catholics was a great embarrassment to Franco's Christian Crusade. In several months of intense fighting, ending in October 1937, the Nationalists overcame the resistance of the Loyalists in the north, and Republican Spain was reduced to a single entity encompassing slightly more than two-fifths of the country, roughly the northeast and southeast regions.

In the meantime, during the relative lull in fighting elsewhere, the Republicans completed the basic organization of their army as an effective fighting force. The struggle for Madrid had precluded an efficient mobilization of resources, but it was during this fighting that an army slowly evolved from the various militias and the mob behind the barricades. The paycheck was one of the principal tools. Until the end of 1936, the government paid militiamen ten pesetas (about $1.20) a day, primarily to help them support their families. A decree of December 30, however, allowed only those militiamen who joined mixed brigades and units of the "regular army" to receive pay.

But while the forms and names of units changed, the original political affiliations of the officers and commissars tended to remain the same. The Communist 5th Regiment, for example, although reorganized as the 11th Division, remained Communist in complexion. Similarly, a number of Anarchist militias were "incorporated" in the 14th Division under Cipriano Mera, and the "Trotskyites" of the P.O.U.M. were formed in the 29th Division, the unit with which George Orwell was affiliated during the early months of 1937. The transformation of the militias into units of a regular army was a slow process, however, and as late as April 1937 the army was still largely a collection of independent battalions even though quite a few brigades—including the Internationals—and a few divisions existed. In several instances they were created in the field, as at Jarama.[1]

THE REORGANIZATION OF THE BRIGADES

The Internationals had borne the brunt of the fighting at Madrid, the Jarama, and Guadalajara, and by the spring of 1937 probably seventy per cent of the volunteers who had fought at Madrid during November and December were in hospitals or in their graves.[2] By an order of April 20, 1937, the International Brigades became units of the regular army, and henceforth an ever-increasing number of their replacements were Spanish. Apart from that, the confusion resulting from the transmission of orders in several languages required the reorganization of the Internationals into brigades of the same or similar nationalities or linguistic groups.

Eventually five more or less "permanent" International Brigades assumed their place in the new army, while two others—the CL (150th) and CXXIX (129th)—existed for brief periods. Each brigade was normally composed of four battalions of about 700 men each, with an additional machine-gun unit, mortar section, scouting platoon, aid station, and transportation unit—a total of approximately 3,500 men in each mixed brigade. These, in turn, were grouped into two "International" Divisions, the 35th, first under the command of General Gall, and the 45th, initially under the command of General Lukacz and later under General Kleber. Eventually, the XI, XIII, and XV Brigades were to comprise the 35th Division, while the XII and XIV were in the 45th, but this did not come about immediately. Each division had an artillery battery of medium calibre and a cavalry squadron, and, like every division in the Republican army, one or two Russian technical advisers.[3]

Until their withdrawal from the Spanish war, battalions of the Internationals were shifted from one brigade to another in response to the exigencies of the moment, while new battalions with new names occasionally were created by consolidating existing units. But the general reorganization took place during May and June of 1937. German, Austrian, Scandinavian, and Dutch volunteers in the Thälmann, Edgar André, Hans Beimler, and "12th of February" battalions were concentrated in the XI Brigade. The "12th of February" was composed mainly of Austrian Social Democrats and Schutzbundlers who had fought in the XII Brigade at Teruel and with the XI Brigade in the Casa de Campo and University City. Its four companies were named after victims of the 1934 struggle with the Dollfuss government: Georg Weissel, Koloman Wallisch, Franz Munichreiter, and Josef Gerel. Among the brigade commanders were Hans Kahle and a succession of other Germans, Richard Staimer, Heinrich Rav, and Szinda, then a Hungarian, Otto Flatter, and finally (September 1938—January 1939) an Austrian, Adolf Reiner. During the summer of 1937 Szinda also served as chief of staff of the brigade. The four battalions were renumbered as the 41st (André), 42nd (Beimler), 43rd (Thälmann) and 44th (12th of February).[4]

The XII Brigade lost the Dombrowsky and Franco-Belge Battalions and became largely Italian, drawing Italian volunteers from other brigades. Its four (eventual) battalions apparently were the 45th, 46th, 47th, and 48th. At least one appears to have been all Spanish as early as April 1937, and Pacciardi claims that at this time the Italians could form only two small battalions of three companies each. The XII was the only International Brigade to remain under the command of a non-Communist during most of the war (first Pacciardi, then Penchienati), although two of its battalions (probably the Spanish ones) were commanded by Communists, and the other two had Communist political commissars.[5]

Following their transfer from the XII Brigade early in May 1937, the Dombrowsky and the Franco-Belge (Marty), together with a newly organized Hungarian Rakosi Battalion and two Spanish Anarchist units, the Rojo y Negro (Red and Black) and the Muerte (Death), formed the CL (150th) Brigade which fought at Huesca and Brunete in June and July. It was then dissolved, the Franco-Belge Battalion shifting to the XIV Brigade and the Dombrowsky forming the nucleus, as well as providing the name, of a reorganized XIII Brigade.[6]

When the reorganization of the Internationals commenced, the Tschapaiew (8th) Battalion of the XIII Brigade was remembered as the 49th, while the other battalions of the brigade (Vuillemin, Juan Marco, and Otumba) were designated the 50th, 51st, and 52nd. As so constituted, the XIII Brigade fought at Brunete in July 1937 and was then reorganized. The Tschapaiew Battalion appears to have been transferred to a CXXIX (129th) Brigade along with the Dimitrov (from the XV) and, together with newly organized Masaryk (Czech) and Djakovitch (South Slav) battalions, briefly fought in the 45th Division under General Kleber in the Belchite campaign of August–October. There is little information about the CXXIX Brigade. _Épopée_ (p. 248) merely lists it, but there is no mention of such a brigade in General Rojo's comprehensive roster of the units participating in this or any of the other military operations of the war. It is known that the Dimitrov left the XV Brigade midway through the Belchite campaign in the late summer of 1937, but just where it went is uncertain. At the time of the Ebro offensive in July 1938, the XIII Brigade still consisted of the 49th, 50th, 51st, and 52nd Battalions, identified as Polish, Balkan, and Czech. While no evidence positively identifies the battalions by name, available information suggests that they included remnants of the Dombrowsky, Rakosi, Dimitrov, Masaryk, Djakovitch, and Tschapaiew. It is quite likely that by this time several battalions had been consolidated.[7]

The XIV Brigade became predominantly French, retaining the Henri Barbusse, apparently renaming the Domingo Germinal as the Vaillant Couturier, and drawing the veteran Commune de Paris from the XI Brigade (after Guadalajara) and the Henri Vuillemin from the XIII (after Brunete). In addition, the XIV seems to have incorporated the remnants of the Franco-Belge (Marty) from the CL and the "6th of February" from the XV (both after the summer offensive at Brunete), and somewhere along the line also acquired an entirely new battalion, the Pierre Brachet. The Commune retained its identity, but the Pierre Brachet, for example, was probably created from the depleted ranks of one or more of the earlier battalions, including the original 12th (Ralph Fox).[8] By the time of the Ebro offensive in July 1938, the XIV Brigade apparently had only the standard four battalions: the 53rd (probably the Commune), the 54th, the 55th, and the 56th.[9]

During the spring of 1937, enough volunteers arrived from the United States and Canada to rebuild the depleted Lincoln Battalion and form two additional battalions in the XV Brigade. One, the Washington, was organized and trained at Albacete and Madrigueras and took up reserve positions at the Jarama in the middle of June. Its first commander was a Yugoslav-American, Marko Marković. The other was formed the last week of June and trained under the command of Robert Merriman, now recovered from the wounds received at the Jarama. Half of the Americans in the battalion wanted to name their unit after Patrick Henry and the other half after Thomas Paine. While they bickered, Canadians, about one-third of the unit's volunteers, submitted and secured the name Mackenzie-Papineau in honor of two nineteenth-century fighters for independence from Britain, one of whom was the grandfather of the then Prime Minister of Canada.[10] However, the battalion did not join the brigade until the fall of 1937.

The XV Brigade was further strengthened by the rebuilding

of the British Battalion, the first company of which adopted the name Major Attlee Company in honor of the leader of Britain's Labour Party, and also incorporated a Spanish battalion, the 24th. Eventually, the XV Brigade was to include the British (57th) Battalion, the Lincoln (or Lincoln-Washington, the 58th), the Spanish 59th (the successor of the 24th), and the Mackenzie-Papineau (the 60th). At the time of the Ebro offensive in the summer of 1938, the five "International" Brigades thus counted twenty battalions, the 41st (André) to the 60th inclusive.

On the eve of the last action at Jarama, a group of some 40 Americans, 50 Englishmen, and 300 Frenchmen, Austrians, Germans, and Poles were organized in a special battalion, the 20th. After five weeks of training the unit was sent to Pozoblanco on the southern front, where, as noted previously, it fought in the Spanish 86th Brigade until June. The commander of the battalion was an Italian, a Major Morandi, and the political commissar a Hungarian Communist, Ferenc Munnich, whose real name was Istvan Toempe. A 24-year-old American Communist, John Gates, who was to be the last editor of the *Daily Worker*, first served as political commissar of the Anglo-American company, then was promoted to battalion commissar and commissar of the 86th Brigade. After three months of service on the southern front, the 20th Battalion returned to Albacete and its members were transferred to other units of the International Brigades, mostly those in the XV.[11]

In addition to the Anglo-American Company of the 20th Battalion, two other groups of Americans fought in Spain. One was the John Brown Artillery Battery, which served for about a year on the Toledo and Levant fronts after it was organized in April 1937, and the other was the 1st Transport Regiment of what became the V Army Corps. In the summer of 1937

87

there were also 25 American hospital units in Spain staffed by 220 doctors and surgeons, 550 nurses, and 600 ambulance drivers, stretcher bearers, and aid men. All were under the direction of Dr. Irving Busch.[12]

This, then, was the organization of the International Brigades as they took shape just prior to the Brunete offensive in July 1937. By this time, except for the Americans and to a lesser extent the British, most of the foreigners inclined to volunteer had already done so. Since the brigades were used as shock troops in virtually all of the major offensive and defensive operations of the war, they were kept at full strength only by incorporating increasing numbers of Spaniards.

THE VOLUNTEERS

From the outset of the civil war until September 1938 when the Spanish Government agreed to withdraw the foreigners serving in its armed forces, some 35,000 volunteers, possibly a quarter of them French but altogether representing fifty-three nationalities, joined the International Brigades.[13] Between October 1936 and February 1937, probably 15,000 Internationals joined the brigades and another 15,000 or so joined before the end of the year.[14] Casualties were very heavy, averaging 15 per cent a month or 180 per cent a year, and after the first big influx of volunteers late in 1936, greatly exceeded the rate of non-Spanish replacements.[15] Only about 8,000 volunteers were in the line in May 1937, and the maximum number of Internationals at the front at any one time could not have exceeded 15,000 and this just prior to the Republican offensive at Brunete in July 1937.[16] During the first half of 1938 probably no more than 6,000 non-Spanish volunteers (at the very most) entered the International Brigades. Given about 700,000 as the maximum strength of the Loyalist Army, the Internationals thus accounted for no more than about two per cent of the Republican forces during the first year of the war, and a considerably smaller percentage thereafter.

Most of the Europeans and perhaps a majority of all volunteers had some military experience prior to the Spanish conflict, but many were thrown into the fray at Madrid and the Jarama, and to a lesser extent at Guadalajara, with little or no training. Nor was the equipment of the volunteers particularly good, although apparently they did receive the best available, including material from abroad.[17] Nevertheless their spirit and zeal saved the day for the Republicans on more than one occasion.

Many volunteers were from those strata of society not particularly concerned with Robert's *Rules of Order*, and such types could be expected to run afoul of the authorities. One young English volunteer, sentenced to a work battalion for desertion, wrote to Stephen Spender about a gang of razor-toting Scots who "could throw a piece of orange peel in the air, spit, and hit it. They drank heavily, passed out, and then drank again." Another English volunteer, Esmond Romilly, who was eighteen at the time, was quite impressed by a group of his countrymen at Albacete whom he knew to be excellent soldiers simply because they cursed everyone and everything. One complained that they had been "waiting about and eating and then waiting about for the next bit of grub. Then they've started some jolly game of hauling ourselves out at six in the morning to go on parade and listen to some fat bastard [André Marty?] gassing his head off in some language we don't understand."[18]

During November and December of 1936, André Malraux recalled that "in spite of every precaution, an extraordinarily motley collection of recruits was arriving for the various International contingents . . . On one occasion, all the hobos of Lyons had set out to join the Brigade, only to be stopped at the frontier and returned to the station they started from. The Brigade was made up of men who could fight, not 'extras' from a film studio." Similarly, the English volunteer Sommerfield complained of "a minority almost wholly irresponsible, often drunk and disgusting," who were sorely resented by the other volunteers. And Sandor Voros later encountered "bad elements at Albacete," the "crippled, ill, shell-shocked wrecks" of the early volunteers who stopped Franco at Madrid—"the multitudes found in every society since the dawn of history who were born to the dry teat and destined for the bottom of the heap."[19]

Wintringham asserts that "the usual 'sanctions' of military discipline were not there; jailing men was too wasteful of time and goodwill for us to do much of it, and we never shot a volunteer that I know of (except Commandant L.). Discipline therefore had to be maintained by our political work; and I wish I knew how it was done." But Longo points out that because of the diverse politics, temperament, and attitudes of the volunteers, it was not always possible to "persuade" and "make acceptable the general interest" without decisions "based on the weight of authority." This is hardly surprising for a military organization, but he also cites the problem of out and out jealousy between various international units. Fraternity among the volunteers was never strong enough to sustain a "solid" military organization, he claims, and "strong discipline" was therefore necessary to weld the diverse elements together. This was necessitated in part by the efforts of "Fascists" and "Trotskyites" to exercise a disruptive influence among the Internationals, efforts which, if we are to believe Longo, were not entirely unsuccessful.[20]

Considering the circumstances of their organization, however, the Internationals performed surprisingly well. The first brigades especially were merely counted off and thrown directly into battle without any time to achieve cohesion, and with the men in the ranks scarcely knowing the names of those standing next to them. One can hardly avoid the suspicion that many of Longo's "disciplinary" measures had political rather than military aims.

The Internationals on the whole seem to have enjoyed considerable popularity with the Spanish people. The exception, an important one, involved their relations with the Anarchists. The German Communist Franz Dahlem claimed that when the XI Brigade was transferred to Murcia in southern Spain in January 1937 to recuperate from the bitter struggle at Madrid, "the population at first gave it quite a cold reception." This was overcome, he maintains, by dances, dinners, and big get-togethers.[21] Anarchist influence was quite strong in the area, and Murcia was rather far removed from any of the military operations. The XI Brigade was one of the best units in the Republican Army, and its exploits were fully appreciated in those areas—Madrid and Aragon—where it saw heavy action.

Some of the Internationals appear to have been more popular than others; the Italians of the XII Brigade and the Americans and English of the XV Brigade seem to have maintained particularly good relations with Spanish soldiers and civilians. "I still marvel at the fact that the Italians seemed to suffer from no feeling of oppression or exile," Regler recalled;

> they truly were on the road to Rome. With all the other contingents—the Germans, readily obedient in their masochism, the melancholy-virile Poles, the eternally grumbling French—I was never sure how long they would put up with the weakness of the Spanish, the amateurishness of their leadership, the defeats and long periods of inactivity. They were

91

never quite at home, perhaps also because the leadership was so largely Communist.[22]

The Internationals organized and supported a number of homes for children orphaned by the war. Apparently as many as 2,000 were cared for "in the loveliest homes, abandoned by Fascists." Probably a dozen or more homes and hospitals were supported entirely by the Internationals or in cooperation with other groups and agencies, including foreign parties. Yet even in these centers, the children were not free from exposure to political ideologies. Thus a children's hospital established and supported by the Internationals at Denia was known as the "Nino Nanetti Children's Home," while a refuge established by the XI Brigade at Moraleja bore the name "Ernest Thälmann Children's Home." A hostel established for 330 children in Murcia was named for General Lukacz, while an orphanage established at Benicasim was called "Villa Beimler." One sponsored by tthe Internationals at Benisa was given the name "Solidarity" to commemorate the fact that the International Brigades "brought together for the first time all Anti-Fascists: Socialists, Anarchists, Republicans and Communists."[23]

As for the Americans, John Gates cites one case in Madrigueras where the volunteers put on a show for the children of the town, bought them toys, and so forth. The climax of the performance came when a burro was led down the aisle of the rented movie house and up onto the stage: "from then on, the town was ours." Commenting on another similar party (or, hopefully, merely editorializing), the *Volunteer for Liberty* mentioned "more than 300 [children], girls first, boys after, singing the 'International,' shouting the 'Young Guard,' happy, untrammeled." The children, we are told, also received toys, cakes and sandwiches.[24]

A majority of the volunteers were Communists, but it is impossible to say how much of a majority. The Communist organizers of the brigades claimed that the Germans were almost entirely Communists; the French and Italians Popular Frontists with "a great majority of Communists in their groups"; the Austrians mostly Socialists; the Poles, Bulgarians, and Czechs mostly Communists; the English Communists, Labourites and Liberals; and the Americans and Canadians "democrats with an important Communist nucleus."[25] Except for the Americans, whose Communist representation was deliberately understated for propaganda purposes, this seems a fairly reasonable assessment, although there may be some question as to whether a "great majority" of the Italians in the XII Brigade were Communists. The English Communist William Rust maintains that most British volunteers were workers whose politics were "left wing and Communist," but others were moderate and liberal, while the views of some could hardly be defined at all. Another ex-Communist who recruited volunteers in England and Wales claims that more often than not they had no political background whatsoever! Herbert Matthews says that a large majority of the volunteers were Communists but a "goodly proportion" were democrats, Socialists, and liberals.[26]

We have it on the authority of John Gates that between seventy-five and eighty per cent of the American volunteers were Communists, probably as high a proportion or higher than among most of the national groups. As Gates points out, since it was illegal to go to Spain, recruitment and transportation were organized on a secret and conspiratorial basis, almost exclusively through the American Communist apparatus. The only exception was a Debs Column organized by the Socialist Party[27] and a few individuals who went to Spain on their own. Unquestionably many genuine democrats who were not Communists would have liked to volunteer for Spain but didn't know how. Gates met many such people in subsequent years.

Those who volunteered through the Communist apparatus were overwhelmingly Communist or close sympathizers. The ratio among the Americans was higher than with the British, where the Labour and Liberal Parties were fairly well represented. More Socialists and non-Communist French trade unionists volunteered, and among the Italians there were significant numbers of Socialists, Anarchists and Republicans. Virtually all key positions among the Americans were filled by Communists, and the Veterans of the Abraham Lincoln Brigade followed the Communist line after the war was over. The Party would have preferred to have more non-Communists, but the manner in which men were recruited made that impossible. André Marty's statement that the Americans were "democrats with an important Communist nucleus" was propaganda to help American Communists combat charges at home that the XV Brigade was predominantly Communist.[28]

Communists everywhere of course exhibited the greatest enthusiasm in recruiting volunteers. General Krivitsky claimed that the majority (but not all) of the volunteers were recruited by Communists and were drawn from a "spreading network" of fellow travelers who quite often were completely unaware of the control which the Communists exerted over them. He also claims that in all countries the recruits were investigated by N.K.G.B. agents who weeded out those Communists whose opinions were not strictly orthodox, i.e., were "Trotskyite" and "deviationist" rather than Stalinist. Krivitsky also alleges that after a medical examination, the volunteers were interrogated again before entering Spain from France.

According to Gates, there may have been "special cases" in which such checking occurred, but neither in his experience or that of a number of other volunteers was this the general rule, at least during the early months of the war. The English volunteer Esmond Romilly was not questioned about anything until he reached Spain, where a political commissar asked his name, age, occupation, his political affiliation, and reason for coming to Spain. Wintringham also claims that the volunteers were subjected to only the most cursory physical examination in Paris, and Louis Fischer insists that he never swore allegiance to anybody or anything and that as far as he knows nobody else did either. But what apparently was true in late 1936 and early 1937 may have been less true thereafter.[29]

Once in Spain, however, pressure was constantly applied to the non-Communist volunteer to win him over to the Party line. Ex-Communist Jesus Hernández, Minister of Education in the Republican Government, claimed that the Internationals included Communists, Socialists, Anarchists, Trotskyites, liberals, Catholics, atheists, and free-thinkers, but that "our propaganda converted all of them to communists." But this is a gross exaggeration. The Communists achieved their greatest propaganda success precisely by stressing the anti-fascist unity policy of the Popular Front. Despite their machinations behind the scenes, the Communist functionaries in the International Brigades, and in the entire Republican army, consistently preached the necessity of an ever firmer anti-fascist solidarity. "We had preferred that the powerful workers and democratic movements . . . had sent Socialists and democratic volunteers in the same proportion to the number of Communists," Marty wrote in 1937. And Georgi Dimitrov, Secretary of the Comintern, expressed to Louis Fischer the hope that America would send many thousands of volunteers, and preferably more non-Communist than Communists. "We can then build the American Popular Front on the Spanish battlefield."[30]

In a "progress report" of March 1937, Party secretary José Díaz claimed that there were then 249,000 Communist Party members in Republican Spain; 87,600 allegedly were industrial workers, 62,250 agricultural workers, 76,700 peasants, and 22,530 members of the middle classes and professions. Since middle-class and professional people formed a comparatively small proportion of the total population, the ratio of Communists among them must have been higher than in the working classes. This is hardly surprising in view of the attitude of the Anarchists and some of the other left-wing parties. A P.O.U.M. pamphlet of 1937 demanded, "simply as a matter of revolutionary hygiene," that only workers be allowed to carry arms, while the bourgeoisie should be used only for work on fortifications or other "behind the lines activity." It further claimed that the parties "pretending to direct the Revolution" (i.e., the Socialists and Communists) actually had no other goal "than the preservation of the bourgeoisie."[31]

Purely Communist and pro-Soviet propaganda—as opposed to anti-fascist and Popular Front propaganda—had mixed success. At times it could be quite subtle, as in the reported conversation between some children in a hostel and a visiting International, one "Gaston":

> "You French?" a little tot wants to know.
> "No, Spaniard."
> "Spaniard? No!"
> "We are all Spaniards now."
> "But now. Before, you German?"
> The others answer excitedly: "The comrade is not a blond!"
> An older boy approached the problem from another point
> "In your land Fascists?"

Gaston laughs. Then seriously:
"Why don't you ask whether our children are happy, have toys, study, sing . . . ?"
The little girl bursts out: "You Russian!" [32]

At other times it would be ludicrously inept as in the *Volunteer for Liberty* of June 15, 1937, p. 5:

Jean Harlow, well known motion picture actress, died in Hollywood a few days ago. Although she was often compelled to act in insipid or even reactionary roles, she always succeeded in relieving the boredom or vileness of the plot by superb acting. Jean Harlow was one of that little bunch of actors, who for years worked towards the unionization of the motion picture industry. Before her death she saw the craft organized, and in militant action.

And, in the *Volunteer* of July 12, 1937, p. 5:

Soviet butter under the Second Five-Year Plan established for itself on the European market the reputation of being among the world's best. One of the principal tasks of the Third Five-Year Plan is to give Soviet cheese a similar position and to raise the central administration of the Butter and Cheese Industry to a leading place in the People's Commissariat of the Food Industry of the USSR.

During the retreat in Aragon in 1938, *The Volunteer for Liberty*, which was under the editorship of Rolfe in Barcelona, appeared in two-page editions carrying bold-face slogans such as "Do Not Yield an Inch of Ground to the Enemy!" (March 17, 1938, p. 1), "Drive Out the Invaders of Spain!" (March 21, 1938, p. 1), and "Now Is the Time to Strike Back!" (ibid., p. 2). Reflecting upon these admonitions, coming as they did at a time when the whole front was collapsing, Voros comments: "Ed Rolfe . . . gets hysterical in Barcelona and sends us truckloads of two page special editions, one after the other, giving us not news nor information, which we crave, but deluging us, a la Pasionaria, with shrill feminine screams of exhortation fathered by desperate fear." But he adds: "Curiously, that back a—— propaganda lifts the spirits of the men" as their contempt for rearguard generals "explodes into laughter."

The prize for ludicrous propaganda, however, may go to Manuilsky for his speech to the Party Congress in Moscow in March 1939. Commenting on the Spanish Civil War, he cited the case of

> rank and filers like John an English truck driver, who, under heavy fire, brought water to the men who were tormented with thirst; when mortally wounded he said: "If comrade Stalin saw this he would clap me on the back and say: 'Well done, John, you're a fine comrade, John.'" (Thunderous applause)[33]

6

COMMISSARS
AND CHEKISTS

THE FIRST COMMISSARS were appointed in August 1936 in the
5th Regiment, and they were later used in other units of the
regular Republican army and all the International Brigades.
The commissar tended to be more important in Communist
and Socialist units than in Republican or Anarchist units.
Unit commanders and commissars generally were of the same
political belief. That is, Communist commanders had Communist commissars, etc. The commissar was responsible for
the unit to which he was assigned in the event of the inca-
pacitation of the commanding officer, with whom he enjoyed
equal rank, and whose orders he jointly signed "as a symbol
of the unity of army and government." [1]

"The Commissar, the political essence of the most conscious
strata of fighting anti-facists, is the soul of this army. He has
forged it into being," declared the Political Commissariat of
the International Brigades. [2] But nothing could be farther from
the truth. The modern commissar had originated in the Red
Army during the Russian Civil War as a political watchdog
over the thousands of former tsarist officers the Bolsheviks had
to employ. In Spain, where only a few hundred officers had

remained loyal to the Republic, such close supervision was unnecessary—certainly not at the brigade and battalion level. Many of the political commissars would have been far more useful as line or staff officers, while their political role led to divided responsibility of the worst sort and aroused the justified misgivings of moderate Republicans.

"Discipline, organization. Both these things should go together in the art of waging war," warned the Political Commissariat of the International Brigades. "Without an organized army battles are not won. And an army which has no iron discipline, absolute and blind obedience to the orders of the military leadership, is not an organized army." But for the commissars this "discipline" involved a separate chain of command. "We know of cases at present being judged by the Tribunals, of Commissars . . . who, because they received orders from their organization, trade union or political party and orders from the War Commissariat and the two sets of orders did not tally, chose to obey the former and ignore the latter." [3] No mention of orders from military superiors—indeed an article published as late as October 1938 stated clearly that "the commissar will complete his functions without interference from the command." [4]

The commissar was also responsible for organizing and conducting training programs in military tactics and hygiene (normal staff and command functions) and to eliminate illiteracy. The literacy campaign was carried out with considerable zeal and apparently met with fair success. By September 1937 every brigade in the Loyalist army had classes for illiterates, and 75,000 troops reportedly learned to read during that year. The political commissar of the XIV Brigade claimed that when classes were started in the Ralph Fox Battalion, seventy Spanish "comrades" could not read or write. "Now, less than three months afterwards, all of them can sign their names." At the same time, it was considered only natural that "in Franco's army or in any capitalist army . . . the cultural question should be neglected." [5] From a military point of view, however, the time could probably have been spent more profitably in other types of training. The ability to sign their own names wasn't very useful to the Republican soldiers who found themselves in Franco's prisons after the war.

On February 14, 1937, the Political Commissariat of the International Brigades ordered that each battalion and brigade should publish brief but frequent newspapers as vehicles for the Commissars' political and military activities.[6] As a result, the *Volunteer for Liberty* appeared in French, German, Italian, Polish, and English, while individual battalions and even companies had their own "newspapers." Among these were the "Dabrowszczak" and "Zolnierz-Wolnosci" of the Poles, "Elore" of the Hungarians, the "Garibaldino" of the Italians, "Our Fight" of the English, "Dimitrovac" of the South Slavs, "Triebnemen" of the Austrians, "Sturmkolonne" and "Pasaremos" of the Germans, "Vers La Liberté" and "Commune de Paris" of the French, and various other journals, including "Adelante la 13!," "Le Soldat de la République," "La Voz de Sanidad," "Venceremos," and "Salud." As we have seen, however, the content wasn't always too inspiring.

Troop "Information and Education," a legitimate if not particularly vital aspect of training, occupied much of the commissars' time. Albacete instructed them to organize collective discussion in each unit. In so doing they should bear in mind the peculiarities of each battalion, each company, the characteristics of their members,

> whether they are peasants or workers, intellectuals, white collar workers, or soldiers from the reserve. The same lan-

101

guage and methods cannot be used in the different cases. The work must be done from different angles, adapted to the mentality and the general and political education of the soldiers.

The Commissar . . . must talk in a natural manner to the soldiers . . . But talking is not enough. The Commissar is not a gas bag, but an educator, a political leader for his unit. And to educate and lead you must make a profound study of those you are educating and leading.[7]

At the same time the commissars should not "forget for a moment what the combatant *ought* to know," specifically, the strengthening of the People's Front and trade union unity, the peasant and agricultural policies of the Spanish Government, the social origins of fascism and the international policy of the fascist powers—Germany, Italy, Japan, "etc."—and their preparation for war against the U.S.S.R., the example of Abyssinia, the "vacillating, cowardly policy of France and Britain," and the "peace policy" of the Soviet Union and its "magnificent aid to the Spanish people." Brigade and division commissars were to hold weekly meetings for officers to ensure that they were not politically "illiterate," "since a part of them came from the old army." But "a large number of the commanders have a strong sense of dignity which must not be offended. The work must be done in an intelligent way." [8] But even this "troop I and E" work was largely wasted effort. Until the latter part of the war, the Republican Army was composed of volunteers, and most of the Internationals had made their way to Spain with much difficulty. They needed no convincing of the justice of their cause.

The scope and nature of the commissars' functions—particularly their unofficial functions—were not accepted by many non-Communists. After several attempts to limit their influence, Prime Minister Largo Caballero had to resign in May 1937; the Socialist Minister of Defense, Indalecio Prieto, made a similar attempt but was forced out of the government. On April 17, 1937, Largo Caballero had issued a sensational order designed to curb the powers of the Commissariat of War. In his capacity as Minister of War (as well as Prime Minister) he himself would decide upon all promotions and removals, and any commissar whose rank and appointment was not confirmed by May 15 was to consider himself dismissed. Pasionaria immediately countered with an admonition, in the evening paper *Frente Rojo*, "Commissars, stick to your posts!" And the Communists later called Largo's attitude "a crime against army and country." By May 15, when the issue would have come to a head, Largo Caballero, who had refused demands by the Communist ministers Hernández and Uribe to dissolve the P.O.U.M., was out of the government. Subsequently, Uribe claimed that Prieto had participated in the plan to remove Largo and was then made Minister of Defense.[9]

But the new Defense Minister shared his predecessor's attitude toward the Communists. Told that the political commissars had improved morale and on more than one occasion had saved the day during the heat of battle, Prieto asked: "But why must the vast majority of them be Communists?"[10] In the not-mistaken belief that the International Brigades were a Communist stronghold, Prieto issued a decree on September 23, 1937 which stipulated that the brigades would legally replace the Foreign Legion which had revolted in July 1936. They would follow the exact structural organization of other mixed brigades of the Republican Army; the volunteers would be subject to the same military codes as Spanish soldiers; their training would conform to the regulations and instructions governing other units in the army; they would cease to be subordinate to their depot at Albacete as soon as they were attached to tactical units; and the Ministry of Defense could assign officers—including Spaniards—to any of the International Brigades. Henceforth, the authorities at Albacete would "keep a file which will contain all the relevant particulars" concerning the volunteers; fifty per cent of officer vacancies must be filled by promotion from the ranks; and commanders of the Internationals must provide the Ministry of Defense with *all* information relative to officers and cadre so that the Ministry might confirm or reject them in their posts.[11]

Longo, Chief of Commissars of the International Brigades, claimed at the time that the decree merely completed the reorganization of the Internationals which had been going on for months. It was the first document which delineated the "rights" and "duties" of the volunteers and did so "in a way which is completely satisfactory to our soldiers." Gates agrees that the Communists accepted and supported Prieto's decree and recalls many speeches made at the time popularizing and defending it.[12]

But then, in November, Prieto removed more than 250 Communist commissars—none of them, however, from the International Brigades—and also secured the resignation of the Chief of the Spanish War Commissariat, Julio Alvarez del Vayo, a Socialist, but an ardent supporter of the commissar system.[13] The Communists in turn increased their efforts to remove Prieto, and finally forced him out of the government after Franco smashed his way through Republican Spain to the east coast in April 1938. Communist Jesús Hernández, ex-Minister of Education, then became Chief Commissar of the Central Army, and under his aegis the commissar system experienced a considerable revival.

The commissars were responsible primarily for the political

situation in their units and functioned chiefly through education and propaganda. Other and tougher methods were the exception and not the rule. In the two years he was in Spain, Gates served as a commissar on the southern front, at Albacete, and as commissar of the XV Brigade. In that time there was only one execution of an American in the units under his jurisdiction, right after the disastrous retreat in the spring of 1938. There was panic and demoralization, and an order came down from Army headquarters to set an example by executing deserters. An American who had deserted under fire on three occasions was court martialed under regular military procedure, found guilty, and shot. The incident was unfortunate because on the following day the order from higher headquarters was rescinded.[14]

The political commissar did have certain police functions, however; he was specifically instructed to weed out "spies," "defeatists," and agents provocateurs, and was urged to obtain repeated statements of past activities from the volunteers: "It is not possible to carry out a systematic check up too often on all our fighters . . . It is possible that individual comrades will protest because they are being asked for the second or third time already to make statements on their past; but do not let us forget that several fascist agents have been unmasked because on each occasion they made different statements."[15]

The S.I.M., Military Investigation Service, was primarily responsible for counterintelligence in the Republican Army. The International Brigades likewise had an S.I.M., but it functioned as a secret political police, modeled on the Soviet N.K.G.B. From headquarters at Albacete, it operated in close liaison with the Political Commissariat of the International Brigades under the direct supervision of the Soviet adviser Alexander Orlov. The first chief, the Italian Communist

105

Vittorio Vidali, went under the name of "Carlos Contreras" or "Commandante Carlos." The Cheka (from the initials of the original Soviet organization) maintained prisons at Albacete (where one of its principals was the brother of Vladimir Čopic, commander of the XV Brigade), at Chinchilla, and later at Horta in Catalonia when the depot of the International Brigades was moved north.[16] When the secret police seized an individual, the usual charge seems to have been "Trotskyism," but also sabotage, membership in the fifth column, and treason to the Party. If the victim were Italian or German, he might be accused of being an agent of the O.V.R.A.[17] or Gestapo.

The Barcelona "May Days" first brought the Cheka more or less into the open. Traditionally, Catalonia, and in particular Barcelona, were strongholds of the Anarcho-Syndicalists who swelled the ranks of Spain's largest labor organization, the C.N.T.[18] Also important, but numerically much smaller than the C.N.T., was the P.O.U.M., the Workers' Party of Marxist Unification, Communist but anti-Stalinist. At the beginning of the Civil War the Stalinists were extremely weak in Catalonia, though they very quickly merged with and secured control of the Catalonian Socialist Party. During the first week of May, severe fighting broke out between members of the P.O.U.M. and C.N.T. on the one hand, and the Catalonian Socialist Party, police, Assault Guards, and Civil Guards on the other. The resistance was finally suppressed after five days of bitter fighting which left more than 800 dead. The P.O.U.M. was subsequently outlawed and many of its members murdered and imprisoned, including a number of foreigners who had joined the P.O.U.M. militias in Aragon during the early months of the war.[19]

George Orwell, who was in Barcelona at the time of the fighting, recuperating from wounds received while serving with a P.O.U.M. unit in Aragon, was fortunate to escape with his life. Among those killed in the fighting was Camillo Berneri, the foremost Italian Anarchist. Among the foreigners murdered *after* the fighting was Georges Kopp, a Belgian ex-officer serving as a Major in the P.O.U.M.'s 29th "Lenin" Division. The C.N.T. subsequently claimed that as many as 150 foreigners were in a single Valencia prison.

John McGovern, an English Labour M.P., obtained entry into the Cárcel Modelo (Model Prison) in Barcelona on November 28, 1937 and spoke to several of the prisoners. "It was a real prisoners' International . . . They came from France, Greece, Germany, Italy, Austria, Belgium, Holland, Switzerland and South America as well as Spain." There were two International Brigades in Spain, McGovern concluded, one a fighting force drawn from the Socialist movement of the world, the other an international Cheka of paid gangsters sent by the Comintern and consisting mostly of Germans and Italians. Nor were the activities of the Cheka confined to Barcelona. A Dutch volunteer cites the intrigue in an artists' and writers' group in Madrid and the "accident" which befell a Russian girl who was found at the bottom of an elevator shaft.[20]

The circumstances surrounding the disappearance of the P.O.U.M. leader, Andrés Nin, were not known until Jesús Hernández, one of the two Communist Ministers in the Spanish Government, published his story in 1953. Nin, he says, was kidnapped by Orlov and his band of Cheka agents, taken to Alcalá de Henares, and there tortured in an effort to extract a "confession" of alleged crimes. The efforts were unavailing, and he was finally killed after a fake liberation by ten "Gestapo" agents, Germans drawn from the International Brigades. The idea for this ruse, which was designed to "prove" that the P.O.U.M. had links with the fascists, Hernández attributes to

107

Vittorio Vidali. Orlov admits that he did have one of his assistants select, from the German Internationals, a bodyguard of "ten devoted Communists," who "followed me everywhere, with tommy guns and clusters of hand grenades on their belts." [21]

The Political Commissariat of the International Brigades attempted to use units of the Internationals in the fighting against the "Trotskyites" and Anarchist "uncontrollables." Shortly after the conflict broke out in Barcelona, a battalion of the XII Brigade and a battalion from the XIII were sent to take up positions in Tortosa, a C.N.T. stronghold on the Mediterranean about seventy-five miles south of Barcelona. Penchienati, commander of the battalion from the XII Brigade, was then ordered to prepare to move his unit to Barcelona to help "put down" the Anarchists. These orders did not come from the brigade commander, Pacciardi, but from a Spanish major, a Communist who had been put in charge of both Penchienati's battalion and the unit of the XIII Brigade.

Alarmed at the turn of events, Penchienati telephoned Pacciardi, who was in Caspe with the rest of the XII Brigade, and was told not to move his battalion under any circumstances. Penchienati held his ground, despite threats by the Spanish major and the Communist officers of the other battalion, until Pacciardi arrived and had them arrested in the name of General Lukacz. Although Pacciardi did not endear himself to the Communists, Penchienati claims that among the Italian Anarchists in his brigade, Pacciardi's popularity, which was high to begin with, was now even greater, and that his firmness was greatly appreciated by the Spanish General Staff when it learned what had happened. In response to a direct query, Pacciardi later advised the author that after the operation against the Anarchists in Catalonia "I understood the political plots of the Communists, and I placed myself against them . . . During my period of command no crime happened in my Brigade." [22]

Apparently no other Internationals were involved. In his biography, Gates insists that the Americans "did not participate in Spain's internal politics and the P.O.U.M. putsch did not directly affect our units fighting at the front, but we considered the counter measures of the government entirely reasonable." At that time the XV Brigade was in the Madrid-Albacete area, and Gates was on the Cordoba front. All they knew about the affair was the official Communist version in the Communist press and the official government version which also condemned the P.O.U.M. "uprising." At the time they had full faith in those versions and saw no reason to doubt them.[23]

But Marty and others in the Political Commissariat at Albacete exhibited no qualms about demanding the blood of "Trotskyites" and otherwise interfering in internal Spanish politics. Referring to the P.O.U.M., Marty, in one of his many perorations to the Internationals, fumed: "The wretches . . . have sought to break the military unity, the anti-fascist unity, of the Internationals . . . The working class will nail them and their infamy to the pillory for spies and provocateurs in the pay of the bloodthirsty torturers of the people." Nevertheless the events touched off no witch hunts among the Internationals since they had few Anarchists and no Trotskyites in their ranks.[24]

A number of incidents had occurred, however. Recalling his first encounter with Marty at Albacete in October of 1936, Regler asserts that he was first searched for weapons before being ushered into his presence. Marty "was genuinely convinced that many of the volunteers who came to his headquarters were Fascist spies. He . . . did not shrink from conducting day long, soul destroying interrogations or . . . promptly liquidating doubtful cases rather than harm the Republic by what he called 'petite bourgeoise indecision.'" In his initial interrogation of Regler, Marty demanded to see his P.O.U.M. membership card, but with "shameless affability" changed his tactics and made Regler commissar of the XII Brigade. Regler also cites the case of two French volunteers, professed Anarchists, who became shell-shocked in an engagement near El Escorial. He recommended that they be sent to a sanatorium, to which Marty replied that he knew of a suitable place. They were taken to Alcalá de Henares and shot by a "Russian execution squad," apparently at the headquarters of Alexander Orlov. Regler further asserts that in July 1937, Theodore Balk was recalled to Albacete by Marty shortly after Balk's wife, a Comintern agent, fell into disgrace in Moscow. Apparently fearing for his own life, Balk took refuge with Regler in the XII Brigade.[25]

During the Jarama campaign, when Penchienati was given command of the Dimitrov Battalion after its first commander was killed, one Furman, a political commissar, attempted to summarily execute some Poles and a Hungarian. Penchienati claims he was restrained when he tried to intercede, but the prospective victims were rescued by a group of Italians from the battalion's 3rd Company. Apparently at the time of the events in Barcelona, one Rudolf Beckman, a German in an artillery battery, was arrested by political commissars for outspoken criticism of certain happenings in his unit while it was in action. Beckman had sent a report directly to the Spanish authorities in which he said that Marty had ordered four militiamen and a captain shot. Beckman was thrown in prison by the Cheka and an effort was made to extract a confession of personal antagonism toward Marty. In the meantime, a friend of

Beckman, who had been present at his arrest at the Cafe Aquario in Madrid, notified the Spanish authorities who then sent two investigators to Albacete. Beckman was found dead in his cell, a "suicide," and nothing more came of the investigation.[26] This was but one of many such acts which earned Marty the appellation *Le Boucher d'Albacete* (The Butcher of Albacete).

Finally, commenting on Marty's denunciation as a police agent and expulsion from the French Communist Party after the war, Gates called it poetic justice for a man who had condemned so many others with far more serious consequences on much the same fallacious grounds. And "The Peasant," one of the great Loyalist heroes of the Civil War, declared: "I do not apologize for anything I have done . . . [but] the excesses of which I may have been guilty were nothing compared with those of Moscow Communists. I did not slaughter my comrades in arms for disagreeing with my political opinions."[27]

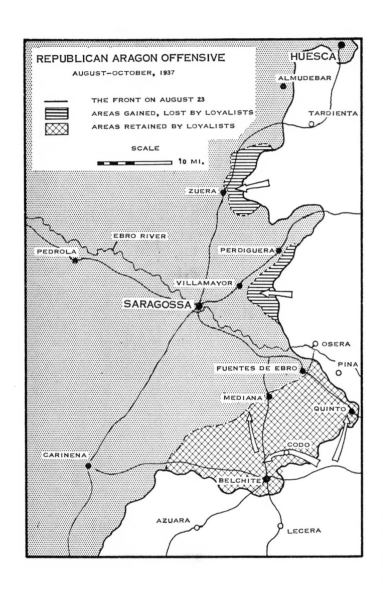

REPUBLICAN ARAGON OFFENSIVE

AUGUST–OCTOBER, 1937

THE FRONT ON AUGUST 23
AREAS GAINED, LOST BY LOYALISTS
AREAS RETAINED BY LOYALISTS

SCALE

10 MI.

HUESCA

ALMUDEBAR

TARDIENTA

ZUERA

EBRO RIVER

PEDROLA

PERDIGUERA

VILLAMAYOR

SARAGOSSA

OSERA

PINA

FUENTES DE EBRO

MEDIANA

QUINTO

CODO

CARINENA

BELCHITE

AZUARA

LECERA

7

BRUNETE AND BELCHITE:
THE FIRST
REPUBLICAN OFFENSIVES

AS WE HAVE NOTED, Largo Caballero was heartily disliked by
the Communists because, among other things, he did not share
their views concerning military strategy. He contemplated an
offensive in Estremadura, in the southwest, and plans were
allegedly worked out by the Spanish General Staff. If successful, such an offensive would have cut Nationalist Spain in two.
The plan was rejected by the Communists, however, who demanded instead an attack west of Madrid, arguing that such an
offensive was necessary to relieve the pressure on the capital.

In retrospect it is doubtful that the Republican General Staff
could have shifted many of their still untrained units to the
southwest rapidly enough to achieve surprise. Too, even if the
attack had succeeded, the Nationalists could still have moved
troops and supplies through Portugal. But an even more important consideration in the minds of the Communists may
have been their fear of the prestige which would have
redounded to Largo Caballero if the Estremadura offensive had

achieved some apparent success. In any event, the Soviet Military Staff declared that no support, least of all aerial support, would be provided for the southern operation.[1] At the same time but for other reasons, the two Communist Ministers in the government—Jesús Hernández and Vicente Uribe—resigned, forcing a crisis. Largo Caballero then quit in favor of a new government headed by Dr. Juan Negrín, a center-Socialist backed by the Communists, and Hernández and Uribe returned. There was no attack in Estremadura, and plans for an offensive against Brunete, west of Madrid, were undertaken in earnest.

In the meantime, two other minor attacks were carried out, the one northwest of Madrid and the second against Huesca in Aragon. The ostensible purpose was to relieve pressure on Bilbao, which was coming under heavy attack from the Nationalists in the north.[2] Had they been carried out in greater strength and somewhat later, the two attacks might have attracted and held some of the Nationalist reserves used during the fighting at Brunete. As it was, they were easily repulsed with local reserves and merely resulted in useless casualties.

The offensive northwest of Madrid had as its immediate objectives the villages of Cabeza Grande, Matabuye, Balsain, and the town of La Granja, and involved only one division, the 35th, under General "Walter," consisting of the XIV and two Spanish brigades, the 31st and 69th. The attack began just before dawn on May 30, but only the 69th Brigade succeeded in taking its assigned objective, Cabeza Grande. The 31st Brigade reached the outskirts of La Granja, but in three days of heavy fighting the XIV was unable to advance against Balsain, and the operation was suspended on June 3. Nick Gillain, who participated in the attack, states that the XIV Brigade lost 900 men, and that the 9th (Commune) and 10th Battalions were particularly hard hit. While inadequate preparation and strength contributed to the failure, Hemingway indicates an additional reason: The enemy, like most of the evening patrons of Gaylord's in Madrid, knew the attack was coming. Hemingway also intimates that Walter may have suffered some interference from André Marty.[3]

Huesca, at the apex of a narrow salient, had been secured by the rebels at the outbreak of the Civil War and had withstood repeated attacks by the Republican militias. The forces committed to the assault on the city in mid-June included the XII Brigade, the CL (150th), under the command of a Spaniard, one Gerassi, and consisting of the Dombrowsky, Franco-Belge, Rakosi and two Catalonian Anarchist battalions, the Muerte and Rojo y Negro, and a Spanish brigade, the 149th (Karl Marx).

Matters took a bad turn at the very outset. The Nationalist Radio Saragossa announced that Internationals were coming to Aragon, and the local Anarchists apparently received them with ill-concealed hostility in some places.[4] And then, motoring to the front before the first shot was fired, General Lukacz and his staff were spotted by the Nationalist artillery. The car in which they were riding received a direct hit; General Lukacz and a Russian Colonel by the name of "Fritz" were killed, and Regler was severely wounded.[5] Shortly thereafter, Pacciardi fell when stepping from his car, twisted his ankle, and had to be carried in a wheelbarrow. General "Belov," Chief of Staff of the 45th Division, momentarily replaced Lukacz, but was in turn succeeded by General Kleber, who had quietly passed from the scene in January.[6]

The attack commenced on June 13 with a fifteen-minute artillery and aerial bombardment. The CL Brigade, supported by tanks, launched the first phase, but failed completely. Leav-

115

ing its positions and advancing across relatively open terrain, the Rakosi Battalion was caught in a withering artillery barrage and subjected to a heavy bombing and in a few minutes suffered over two hundred casualties. Due to a complete lack of artillery and promised tank support, the XII Brigade was unable to even leave its positions. The remnants of the CL fled back to their lines, and further action was suspended for three days.[7] A second attack was launched on June 16, this time with the XII in the vanguard. But without artillery or aerial support, the Internationals and the Spanish units (particularly the Muerte Battalion) were smothered in the Nationalist artillery fire.[8] Casualties were heavy—over 225 in the XII alone, including two battalion commanders. The operation was suspended on June 18, the day before Bilbao fell to the Nationalists, and the "Huesca offensive" came to an ignominious end.[9]

BRUNETE

The first important Republican offensive was designed to relieve pressure on the capital and, if possible, lift the siege altogether. In the first phase, Loyalist troops were to advance south and southeast on an eight-mile front west of Madrid. If they succeeded, another major attack would then be unleashed from the lower Jarama westward, with the objective of meeting the northern prong of the attack at Navalcarnero and thus sealing off the Nationalists in a gigantic trap. In addition, like the smaller attacks on La Granja and Huesca, the offensive was designed to ease pressure on the Republican-held territory in the north, pressure which increased with the fall of Bilbao, and which now was directed at Santander.[10] During May and June upwards of 100,000 troops trained intensively for the attack, and morale apparently reached a new high. "There isn't the slightest doubt but that the Republican forces will win," one young American wrote home. And another: "Put in your order now! Keep a fascist in your back yard instead of a garbage pail! They are guaranteed to be docile and will eat anything. It's the truth."[11]

Approximately 50,000 men in ten divisions and three army corps participated in the opening phase of the well-planned offensive, which commenced on July 6 after an initial diversionary attack at Cuesta de la Reina. Five of the International Brigades (i.e., all except the XIV, which remained at Escorial) participated in the campaign. The XI, consisting of 2,600 men in the Edgar André, Hans Beimler, Thälmann, and "12th of February" Battalions, was assigned to the 35th Division under General Walter. The XII, not yet recovered from Huesca less than a month before, was in reserve together with the CL in the 45th Division under General Kleber, but then went into action on July 7.[12] The XIII Brigade, consisting of the Tschapaiew, Vuillemin, Marco and Otumba Battalions, was attached to the 15th Division under General Gall. In the same division was the XV Brigade, consisting of two provisional regiments, one composed of the Lincoln, Washington, and British Battalions, and the second of the Dimitrov, the "6th of February," and the 24th Spanish Battalion.[13]

Initially, the Republican forces had effective artillery and aerial support, and in just two days they took Quijorna, Villanueva del Pardillo, Villanueva de la Cañada and Brunete; the Nationalists admitted great surprise and "extraordinary anxiety." [14] In spite of its lossess at Huesca, Penchienati's battalion of the XII Brigade scored a particularly brilliant feat in its capture of Villanueva del Pardillo. The Spanish General Staff cited the brigade, much to the annoyance of the Communists, and Penchienati was promoted to major.[15] But even while the Italian Internationals were taking Villanueva del Pardillo and at the very moment elements of Lister's 11th Division were hoisting the Republican flag in Brunete, the attack was beginning to bog down.

The Washington and Dimitrov Battalions had been ordered to infiltrate past Villanueva de la Cañada, while the Lincoln and British Battalions surrounded and took the town.[16] Approaching the village, scouts of the Lincoln observed a steady exodus of civilians and assumed that the town was being evacuated. Word was sent back to the Lincoln and British Battalions, which then advanced only to meet a withering fire from the tower of the village church. The Washington was summoned to help but made the mistake the Lincolns had made at the Jarama, bunching together. Pinned down in a ditch on the outskirts of the town, they remained for several hours in scorching heat without water. The village was finally taken, but at the cost of fairly heavy casualties. This was due in part to the effectiveness of the defenders' fire from the tower of the village church.[17] The British, Lincolns, and Washingtons were then ordered to press the attack past Brunete. After two days of continuous action and with food and water nearly exhausted, the troops reached the foot of Mesquite Ridge on July 9, some eight kilometers southeast of Villanueva de la Cañada and two kilometers west of Boadilla. This was the limit of the Loyalists' advance, and all attempts to dislodge the enemy from Mesquite Ridge were repulsed.

By this time Nationalist resistance had begun to stiffen elsewhere on the front, particularly on the Republican right flank and south of Brunete, where the 108th (Spanish) and XI Brigades of the 35th Division were halted in their drive on Navalcarnero. In the five days between July 12 and 17, neither side made any gain, but the situation changed abruptly on the 17th, when the Nationalists launched a counteroffensive on all sides of the Loyalist pocket. Additional units had been brought down from the northern front (altogether some 40,000 troops supported by 65 artillery batteries, all under the command of General Varela), but the Nationalists most effective weapon was their air force, largely German and Italian. Bombing and strafing in the open, flat country were very effective. Apparently many Loyalist troops had failed to dig in, and General Rojo recalled his feeling of "inferiority and incompetence" when the counterattack got under way. The XIII Brigade, on the left flank of the XV, and other Republican troops around Brunete were caught in the open and subjected to the most intensive and unrelenting aerial and artillery bombardment yet experienced. Several brigades (including, apparently, the XIII) wavered; some units broke in complete disorder and were cut to pieces as they fled from their positions.[18]

The Lincoln and "6th of February" Battalions put up a stiff resistance in retreating from the Mesquite Ridge sector, but were forced to fall back when their ammunition was nearly exhausted. The "Tom Mooney Machine-Gun Company" of the Lincolns fired the last cartridges for its 1914 Maxims, sent the weapons themselves to the rear, and the battalion thus lost most of its firepower. Legionnaires recaptured Brunete on the 24th after a bitter fight with the XI Brigade, which had suffered over 600 casualties; the Lincoln and Washington Battalions had already lost fifty per cent of their pre-battle effectives (including two of three brothers in the Lincoln and Oliver Law, commander of the Washington), while the British Battalion had only 42 of its original 300 men.

The remnants of these battalions were pulled out of the line after the fall of Brunete and literally staggered to the rear past the Spanish relief units. They had been in action for almost three weeks with a minimum of food and water. On the way to the rear the bearded, filthy survivors stopped at a farmhouse (dubbed the "Pearly Gates") to rest, when word came that the Spanish relief was cracking under pressure and that the Internationals were needed back in the line. All of the Americans and 37 of the 42 British survivors (the other five being too sick to even stand) were on the point of returning when word was received that the Spaniards had rallied—they would not be needed. Several of the men then collapsed.[19]

When the battle came to an end on July 28, the Loyalists still held Quijorna, Villanueva de la Cañada (successfully defended by Lister's three brigades, together with the XV), and Villanueva del Pardillo, retained largely by the fierce resistance of the XII Brigade; the lines in this sector then remained virtually unchanged until the closing days of the war. While the first major Republican offensive was not a complete failure, it was very costly in terms of men and materiel. Although it had attracted some Nationalist units from Santander in the north, it failed to achieve its avowed objective of easing pressure on Madrid. Cassado claims that the results of the offensive were entirely negative: with the net gain of territory, the extended lines needed twice as much artillery and infantry for their defense. He also says that the Republicans lost 15,000 in dead alone, but General Rojo maintains that the rebels did not press their counterattack because of their own high losses.[20]

Although it had been well conceived and well planned, execution of the offensive was hampered by the dearth of competent field officers—majors, colonels, etc. As might have been expected, however, the Political Commissariat of the International Brigades concluded that the Brunete campaign revealed that the political commissars had not carried out "special, systematic, well organized work among the commanders and officers," who simply did not prove themselves equal to the situation, i.e., their political rather than their military training was at fault. A shortage of ammunition and planes precluded sustained aerial and artillery support. Too, the obsolete materiel of the Republican artillery was a problem in itself. Colonel Casado claims that after four days of fighting the entire XVIII Corps had only fourteen usable guns. The same defects determined to a considerable degree the outcome of each of the three major offensive operations undertaken by the Republicans during the remainder of the Civil War, Belchite, Teruel, and the Ebro. Each could be roughly summarized in five words: initial success, stall, counter-offensive, retreat.

BELCHITE

The CL (150th) Brigade was disbanded after the Brunete campaign and two of its battalions, the Dombrowsky and the Rakosi, joined by the Dimitrov from the XV Brigade during the Belchite offensive, formed a reorganized XIII Brigade. Three International Brigades were returned to various camps near Albacete for recuperation and reorganization, while the XI and XII were placed in reserve positions near Caspe. By this time the great majority of the replacements in the International units were Spanish; in the case of the XII Brigade, for example, between sixty and seventy per cent.[21] The XV Brigade, however, remained predominantly foreign longer than the others. Although the Lincoln and Washington Battalions were merged as a result of the heavy casualties sustained during the Brunete campaign, the flow of volunteers from the

121

United States, Britain, and Canada continued during the summer of 1937. The Mackenzie-Papineau Battalion, with one Canadian and two American companies, had continued training during the Brunete offensive and was not formally attached to the XV Brigade until early October, after the first phase of the Aragon offensive was over.

Pacciardi made a trip to Paris with Pietro Nenni after the Brunete campaign to discuss, with representatives of the Italian anti-fascist parties, procedures for providing the volunteers with leaves. In his absence, the Political Commissariat at Albacete appointed Penchienati to replace him. Penchienati received formal notice of his appointment on the eve of battle, and *after* it had been fully publicized. Simultaneously, political commissars attempted to foment hostility towards Pacciardi by spreading unflattering inferences regarding his absence during the opening phase of the Guadalajara campaign in March. Penchienati himself protested the move and submitted his resignation, but the Commissariat refused to accept it. At the same time they offered Pacciardi a division, knowing full well that he would refuse it (as he did) on the grounds that he was only prepared to command his Italian volunteers. The rank and file of the XII Brigade were apparently quite bitter about Pacciardi's ouster, and not a few seem to have considered departing with him. The broader issue kept them in the fight, however, and Penchienati (partly on the urging of Nenni) prevailed upon Pacciardi to remain with him—in fact, very close to him—until the termination of the Belchite offensive. He felt Pacciardi's presence would boost morale, but he also feared that agents of the Cheka might make an attempt on his life. During the battle, Pacciardi held a staff post and later made a propaganda tour in the United States on behalf of the Spanish Government.[22]

Bilbao had fallen to the Nationalists on June 19, and the situation in the north was even more serious in August. Hence the Republicans second offensive, in Aragon, was designed, in part, to force the Nationalists to withdraw troops from their attack in the northern coastal provinces. The objectives were Codo, Quinto, Belchite, and Fuentes de Ebro southeast of Saragossa, Zuera to the north, and the provincial capital (Saragossa) itself. The capture of Saragossa would also put the Republicans in a much better position from which to undertake an assault on Huesca.[23]

Approximately 75,000 Republican troops in two corps, eight divisions, and six independent brigades participated in the operation, which commenced on August 24. The XI, XII, XIII, and XV Brigades led the attack, along with Lister's 11th and Campesino's 46th Divisions. The Spanish 27th Division assaulted Zuera with great initial success, while General Kleber's 45th "International" Division, consisting of the XII and XIII Brigades, proceeded with difficulty against Perdiguera and Villamayor, northeast of Saragossa. South of the Ebro, while the XI Brigade was taking Codo, the Lincoln, Dimitrov and 24th [Spanish] Battalions assaulted Quinto, which was finally taken with the help of the Spanish 32nd Brigade after two days of bitter fighting.[24]

The front between Belchite and Quinto was completely broken, and some disorder among the Loyalist troops resulted from the rapidity of their advance, which was led by tanks, and from inadequate communications. The XV Brigade advanced to within two miles of Fuentes de Ebro, but all efforts to take the heavily fortified town were unavailing. In the meantime, Belchite had also withstood the assault of the Republicans, so the XV and 32nd Brigades were shifted to that sector. The new commander of the XV, Hans Amlie (formerly the battalion commander of the Lincolns) was wounded in the attack, as was the new commissar, Steve Nelson. The Americans sustained relatively heavy casualties in fighting Hemingway called "the sort you never know whether to classify as hysterical or the ultimate in bravery." Belchite finally capitulated, after house to house fighting, with the surrender of some 1,500 Nationalist troops on September 3.[25]

While the XV and 32nd Brigades were assaulting Belchite, the rest of the V Corps was attempting to advance northwest in the direction of Saragossa. The attack stalled in the face of mounting resistance, however, and the Republicans were forced to dig in and consolidate their positions. Simultaneously, the XII and XIII Brigades of the 45th Division, after suffering very heavy casualties, were stopped just short of Villamayor, and the 27th Division, after its initial success, was unable to take Zuera.[26] The steam had now gone out of the offensive; tank attacks stalled, infantry assaults were uncoordinated, and in the course of a month's fighting the 27th and 45th Divisions were forced to retire to the positions north of the Ebro held at the start of the offensive. But even when the initial offensive had spent itself, the Republicans were able to hang on to virtually all of their gains south of the river. They still had not succeeded in taking Fuentes de Ebro, however, and after a period of relative calm, a concerted attack was again launched on the town on October 13. The Mackenzie-Papineaus, in their first action, and the Lincolns led the assault. But as on so many previous occasions, aerial support was not forthcoming, and the preparatory artillery barrage was scattered and ineffective. The attack failed and cost the "Mac-Paps" fairly heavy casualties.[27]

On October 22 news was received that the Nationalists had completed their conquest of the Asturias, thus reducing Republican Spain to a single entity, and the decision was made to suspend further action in Aragon. On October 24 the lines were stabilized with the Loyalists in possession of the greater part of their initial gains including Belchite. But Saragossa remained in enemy hands. While the second phase of the struggle for Fuentes de Ebro was raging, the Nationalists attacked at Cuesta de la Reina (Sesena), south of Madrid, in an attempt to take Aranjuez. The XIV Brigade was thrown into the defense, and the rebel drive was halted, but at a cost to the Brigade of 1,000 casualties between October 16 and 25. Casualties sustained by both sides in the whole of the Belchite campaign are not known. Aznar (p. 486) contends that the "Reds" lost 20,000 men by September 15. Hemingway placed total Republican casualties at 3,000 and Nationalist casualties at 7,000, but both of these figures appear much too low.[28]

During one of the assaults on Fuentes de Ebro, a "new tactic"—the armored column breakthrough—was attempted. John Gates claims that a hundred tanks (the largest number assembled by the Loyalists during the entire war), manned by Slavs with Spanish troops riding on top, spearheaded the attack, followed by British, Canadian, and American infantry, in a dash for Saragossa. The tanks apparently advanced so swiftly, however, that the supporting infantry, as well as that of the enemy, were left far behind. The tanks "were cut off and finally destroyed or captured." The failure of the operation Gates attributes to a breakdown of communications, which in turn resulted from the multiplicity of languages involved in the transmission of orders.

Penchienati tells us that in the 45th Division General Kleber's insistence on giving all orders verbally in Russian led to a tremendous amount of confusion. When the situation began to deteriorate, Kleber attempted to shift the blame and ordered the summary execution of a battalion commander of the XII Brigade, Raimondi, interestingly enough a "pure" Communist. Before Raimondi could be executed, however, Kleber was replaced by Hans Kahle ("Colonel Hans"), who had commanded the Thälmann Battalion during the struggle for Madrid, and later, the XI Brigade at Guadalajara. Kleber then disappeared from the scene and was not heard of during the remainder of the war, while Raimondi was promoted to major.[29]

On one occasion, a concerted attack on Saragossa itself was planned, zero hour was set, and the troops were deployed for the assault. Just a few hours before the attack was to commence, however, the Loyalist staff officer who was largely responsible for its preparation deserted to the Nationalists with the complete plans of the operation. His presence allegedly was missed by a political commissar who immediately gave the order to scatter the troops from their points of concentration. The redeployment was effected in the nick of time, as shortly before zero hour, waves of German and Italian bombers appeared and saturated their original positions with bombs.

General Rojo contends that a principal cause of the failure of the offensive was the inability—or reluctance—of the 27th Division to fulfill its part of the operation. Penchienati supports this, but also claims that the bad blood which developed between the XII and XIII Brigades over the Barcelona May Days resulted in a few brushes during the attack against Villamayor. But, as before, the principal Republican defects were insufficient planes and artillery and poor command of the troops in the field. Rust quotes General Walter (commander of the 35th Division) as saying: "Discipline and order in the various units were poor. This was hardly surprising. The American comrades, who became a very important factor in the reorganization of the Brigade, had at that time almost no military experience and training." This was at least true of the Mac-Pap Battalion.[30]

The rank and file of the Republican troops fought hard and well in the Aragon offensive, but their bravery was matched by that of the Nationalist troops, who also had officers capable of making their technical superiority pay off. Nevertheless, the Loyalists did gain a modest amount of territory and learned a few more lessons which they shortly put to advantage in one of their two great operational accomplishments of the war—the winter battle at Teruel.

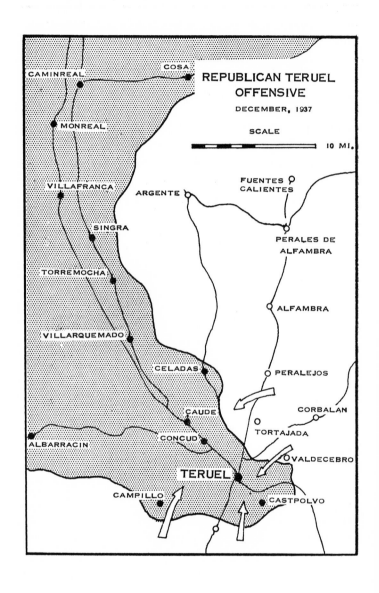

REPUBLICAN TERUEL
OFFENSIVE

DECEMBER, 1937

SCALE

10 MI.

CAMINREAL

COSA

MONREAL

VILLAFRANCA

ARGENTE

FUENTES
CALIENTES

SINGRA

PERALES DE
ALFAMBRA

TORREMOCHA

ALFAMBRA

VILLARQUEMADO

CELADAS

PERALEJOS

CORBALAN

CAUDE

TORTAJADA

ALBARRACIN

CONCUD

VALDECEBRO

TERUEL

CAMPILLO

CASTPOLVO

8

TERUEL TO THE EBRO: THE INTERNATIONALS' LAST BATTLES

DURING NOVEMBER 1937 Republican intelligence discovered that General Franco was gathering forces for another assault on Madrid.[1] It was therefore decided, as a counter measure, to launch a major offensive against Teruel. The city, at the apex of a potentially dangerous salient protruding into Republican territory, had been seized by the rebels the day the Civil War commenced and remained in their hands despite a series of attacks in which the XIII Brigade participated in December 1936 and January 1937. The new offensive, prepared by Colonels Rojo and Hernández Sarabia and executed under the direction of the latter, was launched on December 15, 1937 in a fifty-mile-per-hour blizzard at a temperature of eighteen degrees below zero. Not one of the 40,000 men participating in the attack, nor of the 50,000 held in reserve, was an International. In accordance with the wishes of Defense Minister Prieto, the offensive against Teruel was an all-Spanish operation, and it was a smashing success. The city fell to the

Loyalists on December 21 after extremely bitter house-to-house fighting.

The capture of Teruel was the occasion for great celebration in Republican Spain, but the very magnitude of the triumph and the prestige which the Loyalists gained as a result made it incumbent upon General Franco to retake the city at all costs. To this end, eleven of the best Nationalist divisions, altogether some 130,000 troops, supported by 100 artillery batteries and perhaps as many as 400 German and Italian planes, were thrown into a counter-offensive which began in earnest on January 7.[2] In anticipation of the counter-offensive, two of the International Brigades, the XI and the XV (in the 35th Division) were sent into the line and went into action near Alfambra on January 5. The bitter fighting which ensued in the course of the next month was made even worse by especially bad weather.[3] When the Nationalists recaptured Teruel on February 23, the XV Brigade, and particularly its Mackenzie-Papineau Battalion, was but a shadow of its former self. During one day the third company of the Mac-Paps lost forty-five of its fifty men. And one battalion of the XI Brigade was almost annihilated when it deployed on a prominence known as *La Muela* on which the Nationalist artillery had zeroed in.[4]

"Campesino's" 46th Division also was thrown into the defense of Teruel and finally had to fight its way out of the town after being completely surrounded. The Peasant claims that the Communists were willing to deliberately sacrifice Teruel in order to "torpedo Prieto." The capture of Teruel had greatly enhanced the prestige of the Minister of Defense, and as long as his influence remained intact, the Communists could not hope to gain complete control of military affairs. According to the Campesino, the first step was to remove Hernández

Sarabia, who had directed the capture of Teruel and who was a close personal friend of Prieto. Allegedly he was transferred elsewhere and replaced by Communist Juan Modesto at the urgent request of the Soviet advisers, Generals "Gregorovich" and "Barthe." The second step was to stop the flow of supplies to the Anarcho-syndicalist units which were holding advance positions, and in particular to deprive them of any heavy artillery support.[5]

Yet, even if what the Campesino says is true, it is doubtful that the Republicans could have retained Teruel, even if its defense had remained in the capable hands of, say, Hernández Sarabia, and had not been compromised by the Communists. The loss of the provincial capital was a terrible blow to General Franco, and there is little doubt that he would have used whatever forces were necessary to recapture the town. As it was, Teruel was retaken by the Nationalists by virtue of their superior numbers and materiel. Their artillery was particularly effective, and the Republicans simply could not match their firepower. The offensive did exact a very heavy toll from the Nationalists in terms of casualties. Yet on the debit side the Republican losses were also very heavy, and the heavy expenditure of supplies and materiel, meager to begin with, left the Republicans in such a weak position as to invite disaster.

THE COLLAPSE IN ARAGON

At 6:30 in the morning of March 9, just two weeks after the end of the bitter fighting for Teruel, the Nationalists unleashed what was to be the decisive offensive of the war. The attack was directed eastward along almost the entire front in Aragon from the Pyrenees to Teruel. After the heavy Nationalist losses at Teruel, the attack came as a tremedous surprise to the

131

Loyalists, and when the offensive burst upon them they had only sixty planes, almost no artillery, and only a few units in position to meet the attack. A number of these went into action without rifles for all of their men, and some lacked machine-guns and even hand grenades.

Some twenty-six Nationalist divisions in seven army corps, including 50,000 Italians and 30,000 Moors, supported by more than 800 planes and the largest complement of artillery and tanks yet mustered, shattered the Republican lines in the first three or four days of battle. North of the Ebro River the offensive completely pulverized the Loyalist X, XI, and XII Army Corps, which had no more than seventy per cent of the men and only about forty per cent of the equipment normally considered necessary for units of their size. The V, XXII, and XXI Army Corps, which bore the brunt of the assault south of the Ebro, were in much the same condition.[6]

When the offensive began, the XI and XV Brigades were deployed in and around Belchite. The Lincoln and Mac-Pap Battalions were charged with the defense of the town itself, but were forced to withdraw late in the afternoon of March 10 after bitter house-to-house fighting. But in comparison with the fighting that followed, the struggle in Belchite was at least a relatively organized affair. Isolated from their divisions and corps, many brigades and battalions were either surrounded and slaughtered or fought their way out of one trap after another. Alvah Bessie recalled one instance in the retreat when he and several other men became separated from the rest of the Lincolns and were groping their way around in the dark:

> I tripped over a sleeping man and he sat up and said *Coño!* . . . I strained to see ahead, and then I heard the voices behind, crying *Halto! Los Rojos! Halto! Los Rojos!* and lengthened my stride . . . I could hear the voices plain

now and the rifles, and pistols, and the bullets snapping over-
head . . . Oh, I thought, I'll die; I'm at the end of my rope,
I can't do it, I can't do it . . .

Loyalist resistance degenerated into a chaotic flight to the east,
the pace of the Nationalists' advance in many cases being
limited only by the difficulty of keeping their motorized
columns supplied with fuel.[7]

On March 13 the Loyalist command ordered all units south
of the Ebro to retreat and concentrate in the vicinity of Caspe,
and on the 17th the XII Brigade (from Estremadura)[8] and
the XIV (from the Madrid front) were sent into Caspe to
bolster the defense. They arrived just in time to join the retreat to the Corbera-Gandesa sector in the bend of the Ebro
River. The exhausted remnants of the XV, XI, and XIII
Brigades (the latter more or less attached to the XV Brigade
on March 11) which staggered into Corbera on March 30 were
immediately ordered to take up new defensive positions for
the purpose of making a concerted stand. But of the 550
Lincolns who had resisted the first thrust of the Nationalist
offensive at Belchite, only 100 were left by the time they
reached Corbera; the other three battalions of the XV had
about the same number; while only two battalions of the XI
Brigade—the Edgar André and Thälmann—had more than
a few effectives.[9]

During the next few days of fighting, the swiftest, most confused of the war, only one quarter of the XV Brigade was able
to escape to safety across the Ebro. At one point the British
Battalion marched straight into a deployed Nationalist tank
unit and was almost annihilated. The other International
Brigades, and many Spanish units as well, suffered losses as
severe or even heavier. Robert Merriman, chief of staff since
the Jarama, took command of the XV Brigade (minus the

Lincoln Battalion), while another Californian, Dave Doran, took command of the remnants of the XI together with the Lincoln Battalion. The survivors of the XV and XI Brigades were finally surrounded on some hills just outside Gandesa. An attempt to break out failed, but the Americans managed to repel an attack by a group of cavalry. After dark the survivors split up in groups in an attempt to sneak through the Nationalist lines. One group of thirty-eight, including Merriman and Doran, ran into a patrol which had been sent out to hunt them down. Shots were exchanged and each man took out on his own. One shell-shocked ex-seaman had to be left behind, and only a very few eventually reached safety on the east bank of the Ebro. Neither Merriman nor Doran was among them.[10] On April 12 the survivors of the debacle gathered east of the Ebro. The Lincoln Battalion was reorganized into one company of two platoons—forty Americans and Cubans in one, and thirty-five Spaniards in the other. The arrival of each man who succeeded in getting through the enemy lines and across the Ebro was the occasion of tearful celebration, but some 400 men of the battalion never returned.

In the north the offensive finally came to a halt along a line roughly following the border between Aragon and Catalonia. South of the Ebro, the nationalists reached the sea on April 15. Full of optimism, they eventually opened another offensive on July 15 aimed at Valencia. The attack, directed from Teruel and the corridor separating Catalonia from the rest of Republican Spain, involved an estimated 80,000 men. The Republicans were not taken by surprise, but were ready and waiting at Viver in elaborate fortifications prepared months before. After eight days of fighting the Nationalists lost between 15,000 and 20,000 men and retired from the field on the 25th, the day the Loyalists launched their own attack across the

Ebro.[11] But with its territory split in two parts, the fate of Republican Spain was sealed.

It was inevitable that political heads should roll as a result of the Aragon disaster, and Prieto's was the first to go. After the fighting terminated, "spontaneous" demonstrations occurred throughout Republican Spain with speakers demanding the removal of the Minister of Defense and shouting such slogans as "Down with Traitors." Following such a demonstration in the town of Pedralbes, Prieto wrote a letter to Prime Minister Negrín stating quite bluntly: "That act was, in my judgment, inspired by yourself." [12] Then he resigned. Premier Negrín reorganized the government under the slogan, "To Resist Is to Conquer!" and succeeded in rallying army and people for one more effort. That the Republicans were able to mount another major offensive after the Aragon debacle, with limited resources and in the face of an enemy with vastly superior armament, is striking testimony of their will to win. Those observers who foresaw an early end to the war after the Nationalists' smashing victory in Aragon were wrong in their expectations by almost a whole year.

THE EBRO

The International Brigades were built up to their greatest strength for the summer offensive, but by this time they were overwhelmingly Spanish. Of the 11,817 men in the XV, XIII, and XI Brigades of the 35th Division, only about thirty per cent were foreigners,[13] fifteen per cent in the case of the XIII, and the proportion in the XII and XIV was roughly comparable. Furthermore, most of the Spanish replacements were not volunteers but conscripts—the great majority beardless youths—and a number were ex-deserters and ex-convicts. Alvah Bessie had the job of

> greeting the new "comrades" who had arrived to reinforce us—they were a scurvy lot, ex-prisoners, ex-deserters, weak and unreliable elements that were being rounded up, for by that time the Government was experiencing some difficulties in finding men

> . . . these men and their attitude . . . convinced you for the moment that our situation was truly desperate—or so it seemed . . . But for the benefit of the folks back home the Lincoln Battalion was always intact, and the constant figure of thirty-two hundred Americans were fighting in Spain. We understood why this was necessary, but it did not prevent us from becoming cynical.[14]

Few volunteers were arriving from abroad by this time. In the three months prior to the Ebro offensive, only about a dozen Americans arrived, and seven of these were veterans of the Jarama who had been wounded and invalided home, but who came back to "finish the job." One of the new volunteers was Jim Lardner, son of the writer Ring Lardner.[15]

In July, of the 2,800 or so who had come from America, some 750 Americans remained in Spain. About 200, including several collected from desk jobs, hospitals, and dissolved artillery, transportation, and anti-aircraft units, were assigned to the Lincoln Battalion along with some 500 Spaniards. In addition, about 50 or 60 Americans were with the Mackenzie-Papineau Battalion and another dozen or so with the British and Spanish (24th) Battalions of the XV Brigade. Another two dozen were serving on the brigade staff, about 200 were serving in various medical and transportation units, and approximately 150 were scattered throughout Republican territory. Of the 70,000 men who participated in the Ebro offensive only about 7,000 at the very most were foreign Internationals.[16]

In spite of the alleged secrecy with which the offensive was prepared and launched (one member of the government claims that the four members of the Supreme War Council did not know of the attack until just a few hours before it began), the Internationals apparently began to suspect something early in June—from their training in river crossing operations, the use of boats, pontoon bridges etc.[17] But not too many of them were enthusiastic, since rumors had begun to circulate that very shortly the Spanish Government would withdraw all foreigners serving in its armed forces. The political commissars had to remind the volunteers that the war went on regardless, and that when the time came for them to leave they would leave—and not before. The Americans in particular seem to have been quite excited about the withdrawal scheme of the London Nonintervention Committee, and while few of them probably had any real faith in the committee, they reputedly "offered as beautiful an example of wishful thinking as you will ever see." The rumors assumed such proportions that John Gates, political commissar of the XV Brigade, had to call a special meeting at which the troops apparently displayed a skeptical and somewhat rebellious attitude.[18]

The offensive launched by the Republicans across the Ebro River on July 25, 1938 had three aims: to divert the enemy from pressing an attack down the east coast from the corridor separating Catalonia from the rest of Republican Spain; to occupy the corridor itself, if possible, thus linking the Loyalist forces in Catalonia with those in the Levante; and finally, to prolong the struggle in the hope that the democracies would

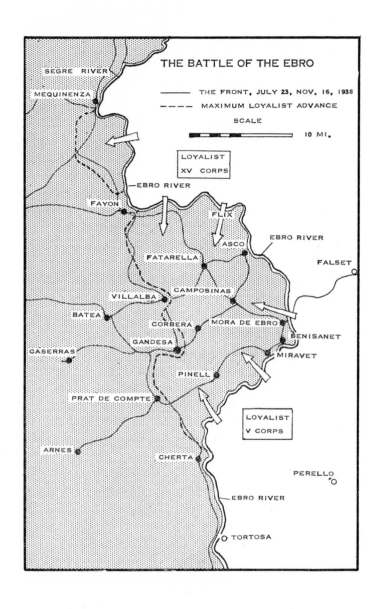

THE BATTLE OF THE EBRO

———— THE FRONT, JULY 23, NOV. 16, 1938

– – – – MAXIMUM LOYALIST ADVANCE

SCALE

10 MI.

LOYALIST
XV CORPS

SEGRE RIVER

MEQUINENZA

EBRO RIVER

FAYON

FLIX

ASCO

EBRO RIVER

FATARELLA

FALSET

CAMPOSINAS

VILLALBA

BATEA

CORBERA

MORA DE EBRO

GANDESA

BENISANET

CASERRAS

MIRAVET

PINELL

PRAT DE COMPTE

LOYALIST
V CORPS

ARNES

CHERTA

PERELLO

EBRO RIVER

TORTOSA

reverse their policies and sell the Republic arms.[19] The assault caught the Nationalists completely by surprise. The XII and XIV Brigades of the 45th Division led the V Corps assault against Benisanet and Miravet, while the XI, XIII and XV[20] Brigades (35th Division) acted as shock troops of the XV Corps against Fatarella, Flix, and Asco to the north. Almost half of the men in the 35th Division who crossed the river did not have rifles, and the entire division counted only 69 machine guns, 38 mortars and four pieces of artillery. Nevertheless, the offensive gained 270 square miles of territory in less than a week, and by August 6, some 500 square miles over a 90-mile front. The Republicans also took 6,000 prisoners. But casualties were very heavy, and the Lincolns had only 400 of their original 700 men by the time they reached the hills overlooking Gandesa on August 6.[21]

This was the limit of the advance, however. The Nationalists threw thirteen of their best divisions into the battle, and by the middle of August the Republican General Staff realized that retirement to their original positions across the Ebro was inevitable. The withdrawal was carried out with considerable skill, and the Nationalists paid dearly for every inch of ground. When the last Loyalists finally crossed the Ebro on November 15, the first snow had fallen in the Levante, and the Nationalists were forced to prepare for another winter of war. But only in terms of one of its avowed objectives—buying time—was the Ebro offensive a success, and even then the hoped for assistance from England and France was not forthcoming.

FAREWELL TO SPAIN

In the meantime, Prime Minister Negrín had flown to Geneva, and in an address to the assembly of the League of Nations on September 21 announced that "The Spanish government . . . having resolved to remove every pretext for casting doubt on the national character of the cause for which the armies of the Republic are fighting, has just decided on the immediate and complete withdrawal of all non-Spanish combatants engaged in fighting on the government side." Premier Negrín followed up his announcement with a request to the League to appoint a commission to supervise the evacuation of the Internationals and satisfy world opinion that the withdrawal was absolute and complete. The British and French representatives at Geneva lauded the withdrawal but suggested that the Nonintervention Committee was better equipped to supervise it. Understandably, the Spanish Government refused to deal with the London committee, and on October 1, the League Council adopted a resolution establishing a military commission, which arrived in Spain on October 14.[22]

In a special issue on September 23, *The Volunteer for Liberty* had officially confirmed the decision of the government, and the Internationals were immediately sent to the rear. Just before dawn on September 24, the last Americans crossed the pontoon bridge at Mora de Ebro, but Jim Lardner, one of the last volunteers to join the Lincolns, and two others who had arrived only a week before, were not among them. Shortly before the battalion was ordered out of the line, Lardner had volunteered to lead a three-man patrol to contact adjacent troops and never came back.[23]

All of the Internationals were back across the Ebro by the end of September and were assembled at various camps in Catalonia to await the arrival of the League commission. Shortly after the commission arrived, arrangements were made for a farewell parade in Barcelona on October 29. Hundreds

140

of thousands lined the flag-decked streets as some 6,000 of the volunteers marched by for the last time in their worn uniforms. The streets were strewn with flowers by a cheering—and crying—populace which well remembered the first volunteers who had departed from their city to help stop the Nationalists in the plains and mountains of Aragon. No doubt a great deal of the emotion also stemmed from the realization, conscious or subconscious, that the war did not have much longer to go.[24]

The League commission, together with the Spanish Government, made arrangements with various foreign governments to repatriate their nationals. In the cases of the Germans, Italians, Austrians, and others who could not return to their native lands, arrangements were made with a number of Latin American governments to admit the Internationals. Mexico, which had rushed 20,000 rifles to the besieged defenders of Madrid in 1936, offered to take 2,000 of the volunteers.[25] The commission allegedly was given free access to all records and information pertaining to the volunteers, and access to all camps, hospitals, and even prisons where the Internationals were to be found. There were 488 in jails at the time.[26] On January 14, 1939, after three months of investigation and organization, the commission announced that 12,763 foreigners of forty nationalities were in the service of the Republic: 7,102 had been in the XI, XII, XIII, XIV, and XV Brigades in their last action on the Ebro, 3,160 were in hospitals, and the balance had been assigned to various medical, transportation, and other service units. In addition, 4,640 had been repatriated earlier by the Spanish Government. The League commission was unable to determine the total number of volunteers who entered Spain, possibly because adequate records had not been kept at the beginning. In its preliminary report, however, the commission insisted that it had been given free and complete access to all information pertaining to the volunteers and was supplied with what it considered "unquestionably authentic" records of the complete history of each combatant. It further claimed that these records "could not have been altered for the purpose of enabling certain volunteers to evade the measures announced at Geneva by the Spanish Prime Minister." [27]

While the commission was organizing the evacuation of the Internationals, the Nationalists launched a concerted offensive against Catalonia which carried to Barcelona itself on January 26. The first large group of volunteers had left Spain on December 21, 1938, but the majority were still awaiting evacuation when Franco's offensive burst upon them. For a while it seemed as though the Nationalists might reach the French border—which was closed by the French Government until February 3—ahead of the retreating remnants of the Republican Army, masses of civilians, and Internationals.[28] As it turned out, the last group of Internationals reached the border, along with the last of some 500,000 refugees, on February 9, just two days ahead of the Nationalists.

Herbert Matthews was at Le Perthus on the French side of the border during the last anxious days awaiting the arrival of the remaining Internationals. Late in the afternoon of February 7 he was standing on a bridge crossing the border, peering down the road into Spain to catch a glimpse of the first elements of the retreating army. A group of Internationals appeared in the distance, not retreating in disorder, but marching as though on parade, flags flying, singing, and with their fists raised in the "popular front" salute. The men passed over the bridge and into France, to be reviewed for the last time by André Marty, Luigi Longo, and Pietro Nenni. And Marty delivered his last speech: "Remember that from now on you

142

will be the guests of France, and you are in no way to cause any trouble. You must maintain your discipline. There is to be no more fist raising, no more singing of the Internationale." [29]

9

WHAT MIGHT HAVE BEEN

"BEFORE MANY YEARS HAVE PASSED," declared Prime Minister Negrín, "their own countries will feel equally proud of the volunteers. That will be their best and highest reward." Although not Internationals, properly speaking, the fate of the Soviet advisers when they returned home foreshadowed the fate of a number of the volunteers from Central and Eastern Europe. In 1938 the *Yezhovshchina,* the Great Purge, was at its worst in the U.S.S.R. Victims were being selected according to quotas, and one of the sure ways of being included in an N.K.G.B. officer's quota was to have lived abroad. Most of the Russians who served in Spain went home to a slow death in a labor camp or, for the lucky ones, a bullet in the neck.

The pattern repeated itself in the "People's Democracies" after World War II. Karol Swierczewski, who as General "Walter" commanded the 35th Division in Spain, became Polish Vice-Minister of Defense and was allegedly killed by anti-Communist partisans in March 1947. He may have been the first victim of the postwar purge. A Colonel Szyr, political commissar of the Palafox Battalion, served in the Polish Ministry of Industry shortly after the war, but seems to have disappeared from the current scene, as has a certain Mietowski, onetime commander of the Dombrowsky Battalion, who became a high official in the Ministry of Security. Tedeusz Oppman, first commander of the Dombrowsky Battalion in the battle for Madrid, served as Polish Military Attaché in Paris after the war, but his current whereabouts are also unknown.

In Hungary, a former Information Officer of the Political Commissariat of the International Brigades, László Rajk, became Foreign Minister shortly after the war, but was executed after a show trial in 1949. Wilhelm Zaisser, General "Gomez," commander of the XIII Brigade and later chief of staff of the International Brigades, was purged in 1953 from his post as Minister of State Security in East Germany. He, too, is now dead. One of Marty's advisers in Spain, Klement Gottwald, became President of Czechoslovakia following the coup of February 1948. He went to Moscow in March 1953 to attend Stalin's funeral and while there succumbed to "pneumonia with complications." His death may have been natural of course. Former Thälmann commissar Franz Dahlem was interned by the French and turned over to the Germans by the Vichy government. Liberated from a prison camp by the Red Army, he became a member of the East German Politburo, Central Committee, and Secretariat, but was charged with the crime of "political blindness" in 1953 and removed. He is now dead.

Former commissar Gustav Regler left the Party after the Spanish Civil War and presently is residing in Mexico. He applied for entry into the United States, but was denied admission because of his former Communist activities. More recently, Alfred Kantorowicz, former commissar of the Tschapaiew Battalion, fled the East zone and sought asylum in the West. One of the very few to survive in Eastern Europe,

Ferenc Munnich, former political commissar of the 20th Battalion, became Deputy Premier of Hungary in 1957 and served as Premier from 1958 until 1961.

The Yugoslavs are in a class by themselves. Tito's activities as liaison officer between Moscow and Albacete removed him from Moscow and probably saved him his life in 1938. Thanks to the partisan apparatus he built up in Yugoslavia, he was able to survive the break with Stalin in 1948. A number of other Yugoslav Internationals survived with him.

André Marty remained in the French Party hierarchy until 1952. Together with former political commissar Charles Tillon, Marty opposed the Party's policy of seeking an alliance with moderate left elements in order to defeat the European Defense Community treaty. Refusing to recant, he was expelled from the Party, denounced as a "police agent," and died in 1954. He has suffered the ultimate indignity of passing almost without mention in the more recent chronicles of his associates (e.g., Longo and *Épopée*).

No purge has yet decimated or radically altered the most powerful, highly organized, and successful Communist party in the West—that of Italy. Yet from time to time in recent years visible strains have developed within the party, in part arising from conflicts between former party leader Palmiro Togliatti on the one hand and the "activist" faction led by his successor, Luigi Longo. After serving as chief liaison officer between Moscow and Albacete during the Civil War, Togliatti survived a would-be assassin's bullet in 1949 and died in a Crimean hospital in 1964. Longo, "Luigi Gallo" when Commissar-Inspector of the International Brigades, was arrested by the Germans in Paris in 1941 but liberated by partisans in 1943. He became vice-commander of the partisan "Volunteers for Liberty" in northern Italy and was decorated by General

Mark Clark. Vittorio Vidali, the "Commandante Carlos" who helped organize the Madrid 5th Regiment, served as Secretary of the Italian Communist Party in Trieste after the war. Eduardo d'Onforio (one of Marty's top aides), Francesco Scotti, a former division commissar, Giuseppe de Vittorio (Mario Nicoletti), commissar of the XI Brigade, and Anelito Barontini, commander in the XII Brigade, all hold or held seats in the Italian Parliament. Under a unique provision of the Italian constitution, Barontini secured his seat in the Senate by virtue of an abortive death sentence passed upon him by a Fascist court.

Of the non-Communists, left-Socialist Pietro Nenni, commissar of the XII Brigade, was interned by the French in 1940, then turned over to Mussolini's government by Vichy, but escaped and took refuge in a Rome convent until the arrival of the allied armies in 1944. Serving for a while as Vice-Premier and Minister of Foreign Affairs until the De Gasperi government undertook a concerted pro-Western policy in 1947, Nenni resigned and aligned his Socialist party with the Communists for several years. He has since joined a majority of his party in supporting the left-center coalition. Former XII Brigade commander Randolfo Pacciardi, dedicated anti-Fascist and anti-Communist secretary of the Italian Republican Party, was decorated while serving as commander of Italian volunteers with the British Army in North Africa. After the war he served as De Gasperi's Minister of Defense from 1951 until 1953.

Of the 2,000 or so Americans who survived the struggle in Spain, some 900 enlisted in the armed forces and merchant marine during World War II. Milton Wolff, National Commander of the Veterans of the Abraham Lincoln Brigade, served with General Donovan's O.S.S. in northern Italy. Several of them, such as former Mac-Pap commander Robert Thompson, came home with more than Good Conduct medals.

A few years after the war, however, several of these men were indicted and prosecuted for advocating the overthrow of the government by force, while others, including Alvah Bessie, were imprisoned for contempt of Congress in refusing to disclose the nature of their past activities. But among the Americans who fought in Spain, they formed a small minority. After an exhaustive investigation, the Subversive Activities Control Board concluded in 1955 that the Veterans of the Abraham Lincoln Brigade had only a few hundred members, and John Gates says that today only a handful of those who returned from Spain are still Communists.[1]

One doesn't have to look far for the reason. In the "Main Resolution" adopted at its first convention in December 1939, shortly after the outbreak of the war in Europe, the Veterans of the Abraham Lincoln Brigade stated: "Let our slogan be: KEEP AMERICA OUT OF THIS IMPERIALIST WAR! THE YANKS ARE *NOT* COMING!"[2] Following the attack upon Russia in the summer of 1941, however, the V.A.L.B. started a campaign to support the Soviet Union. And in 1948 one of the organization's publications followed the Communist line word for word:

> . . . the simple aspirations of the people for security, for decency, for peace. It is these aspirations . . . which the enemy today is attempting to suppress in Greece, in Palestine and Indonesia, in Indo-China, in the Marshall Plan countries and in great China as well as in America itself. And the Spanish people know that the enemy cannot win. The partisans in the Greek mountains grow stronger despite reports of their imminent liquidation. Despite American aid

to the reactionaries of Britain, France, Holland, Belgium and Italy, the people are restless and dissatisfied . . . and the Chinese "bandits" are about to liberate four hundred million people from the tender ministrations of foreign capitalists and quislings.[3]

And immediately following the invasion of South Korea in June 1950, the V.A.L.B. referred to "Syngman Rhee and his clique" as "forced upon the Korean people by American Brass Hats." [4]

Some 300 people, of whom only about 40 had served in Spain, attended a meeting of the organization in San Francisco on April 9, 1967, at which Steve Nelson, onetime commissar of the XV Brigade, was elected national commander. "There may be a few Communists among us," he declared, "but we are not a Communist organization." According to the San Francisco *Chronicle* the next day, however, "most of the speakers condemned America's role in Vietnam . . . *Available near the door were copies of Quotations from Mao Tsetung*" (italics supplied).

Viewing the events in Spain in the total context of the second World War, Salvador de Madariaga observed:

If international Brigades were put together and students in American universities enlisted and died to rescue the Spanish Left on the ground that it fought for Democracy, what less than International Divisions or Armies should have been recruited for England when she stood alone in the world for democracy after Dunkirk? But no. The Communists were not in the business and there was no enthusiasm for England in the world, none even among English Communists themselves.[5]

Señor de Madariaga wrote with some justice, but most of the countries from which volunteers would have come were oc-

150

cupied by German troops after Dunkirk. Even so, within three or four years, a number of Polish and French divisions were fighting or training to fight the Germans. These divisions, of course, were not strictly comparable to the International Brigades, since the Poles and French were serving in what were essentially their national armies. But the Americans who wore British battle-dress after Dunkirk are comparable to the International volunteers in Spain. Only 3,000 Americans served in Spain, but at the time of Pearl Harbor perhaps 1,000 were serving with the British Army and Royal Air Force, while some 10,000 had enlisted in the Canadian armed forces.

Hundreds of foreign volunteers made their way to Spain without any Communist help; thousands would have done so had such help not been available. Unfortunately their idealism and self-sacrifice merely helped prolong the struggle. Given the policy of "nonintervention" adopted in Paris and London, the best outcome for Spain would have been an early end to the Civil War. And if Stalin was supporting the Republic to embroil Britain and France in a war with Germany and Italy, then the irony becomes bitter indeed.

Liberals throughout the world would certainly have welcomed a Republican victory, and the Communists would not necessarily have been able to seize power in such an event. (Indeed, much of their popularity stemmed from the aid furnished by the Soviet Union which the Spanish Government could hardly refuse in view of the Anglo-French policy of "nonintervention.") But how would a democratic republic have fared after the fall of France in 1940? Democratic Sweden found it expedient to allow the transit of German troops and materiel across her territory, and Germany crushed Greece and Yugoslavia in 1941—the latter merely because Hitler mistrusted the Simović government formed after the coup d'etat of March 27. Could a democratic Spain have avoided a similar fate?

During the summer and autumn of 1940, Hitler was seriously considering a German attack on Gibraltar and made every effort to secure Spanish cooperation. Carried out successfully, such an operation would have made the western Mediterranean an Axis lake and prevented the Allied occupation of North Africa and Sicily in 1942-43. Had it been underway in November 1940, the operation might also have induced Stalin and Molotov to adopt a more cooperative attitude, and in December Hitler might not have decided to attack Russia. Admittedly a lot of "might haves," but given Spanish cooperation Hitler would undoubtedly have attacked Gibraltar.

And had the Nationalists taken Madrid and ended the Civil War in 1936, Franco might have been tempted to participate. As it was, however, with half a million dead, a disaffected population, and an economy on the verge of collapse, he had good reason to avoid participating in the war against Britain. He had a long talk with the Führer at Hendaye on October 23, and Hitler later remarked that he would rather have several teeth pulled than have another such conversation. Finally, in December 1940, Franco flatly rejected the attack on Gibraltar. Extension of the British blockade to the Iberian Peninsula, he pointed out, would make Spain completely dependent upon Germany for food and gasoline.

The volunteers of the International Brigades helped prolong a bloody and futile struggle, but paradoxically those who fell did not necessarily die in vain. By preventing an early Nationalist victory, they may have contributed significantly to Hitler's defeat eight years later.

NOTES   BIBLIOGRAPHY   INDEX

Notes

INTRODUCTION

1. Julio Alvarez del Vayo, Republican Minister of Foreign Affairs, subsequently admitted that "there was no doubt about it. The rebellion had surprised the government in the sweetest of slumbers. And, what was worse, even with the aid of such an ear piercing alarm clock, it had difficulty in waking." (*Freedom's Battle*—New York, 1940—p. 21.)

2. *Mundo Obrero,* July 14, 1936, p. 1. See also the speech of José Díaz, General Secretary of the Spanish Communist Party, in the Cortes on July 15, 1936 (*Tres años de lucha*—Bar-le-Duc, 1939—pp. 247-52).

3. Peter Merin, *Spain Between Death and Birth* (London, 1938), p. 165.

4. *Freedom's Battle,* p. 124.

5. A particularly interesting account by an American-born woman resident in Barcelona, who witnessed the assault on rebel sympathizers holed up in the Church of the Carmelites, is that of Megan Laird, "A Diary of Revolution," *The Atlantic,* November 1936, pp. 513-33. See also Part I, Chapter II of *L'Espoir* by André Malraux (Paris, 1937), pp. 15-29, and the English translation, *Man's Hope* (New York, 1941).

6. "Testimony of General Don José Moscardó e Ituarte," *The Red Domination in Spain* (Madrid, 1946), p. 318. The insurgents gathered within the Alcazar included some 100 officers, 800 Civil Guards, 190 Cadets, 200 Falangists and other rightists, and 600 women and children. There were, in addition, and by General Moscardó's own admission, "a num-

155

ber of persons of left-wing politics as hostages." (*Ibid.*, p. 320.)

7. See Major Geoffrey McNeil-Moss, *The Siege of the Alcazar* (New York, 1937). Also Erich Dietrich, *Kriegs Schule Toledo* (Leipzig, 1937).

8. This figure may well be too high, inasmuch as the Assault Guards in several cities (including Huesca, Valladolid, Saragossa, Granada, Leon, Pamplona, and Salamanca) supported the rising. See Burnett Bolloten, *The Grand Camouflage: The Communist Conspiracy in the Spanish Civil War* (New York, 1961), p. 36. Also Capitan Reparez y Tresgallo de Souza, *Desde el cuartel General de Miaja al sanctuario de la Virgen de la Cabeza* (Valladolid, 1937). Prior to joining the rebels, this officer had served in the Assault Guards. In addition, José Munoz Lopez, a high-ranking official in the Republican S.I.M. (Military Investigation Service) advised Bolloten after the war that only some 300 of the government's 3,000-man secret service remained loyal at the time of the rising (Bolloten, p. 36).

9. A Republican navy official claimed that seventy per cent of the navy's officers, that is those who supported the rebellion, were killed by their crews who remained loyal to the Madrid government. Bruno Alonso, *La flota republicana y la guerra civil de España* (Mexico City, 1944) p. 25.

10. *Red Domination in Spain,* exhibit #3, Annex X. For an interesting account of the Military Union, see Antonio Cacho Zabalza, *La union militar española* (Alicante, 1940).

11. Italian Communist Luigi Longo, who subsequently became Chief Commissar-Inspector of the International Brigades, claims that the Republic actually did not suffer from a lack of combatants. These he placed at 150,000 in August 1936, including 20-25,000 professionals from the "old army," 35-40,000 from each of the three workers' organizations (which he labels "Communist, Socialist, and Anarchist," in that order), and 10,000 from the "bourgeois parties" (*Le Brigate Internazionali*—Rome, 1956—pp. 18-22). Prior to the rebellion, however, the Communists enjoyed little success in the labor-union field and had nothing to rival the huge C.N.T. (Anarcho-Syndicalist) and U.G.T. (Socialist). The classic

study of these organizations and their social origins is that of Gerald Brennan, *The Spanish Labyrinth: An Account of the Social and Political Background of the Civil War* (London, 1950, 2nd ed.).

12. Thomas H. Wintringham, *English Captain* (London, 1939), pp. 128-29.

13. Díaz, *Tres años,* p. 401. The organization of the mixed brigades commenced on October 10, but by December 27, thirty per cent of the effectives of the 5th Regiment still remained under the command of that unit. See also "Our Army Is a Peoples' Army," *The Volunteer for Liberty,* vol. 1, no. 2 (June 1, 1937), p. 7; this is one of several sources which claim that the 5th Regiment counted some 45,000 or more members elsewhere in Spain in addition to the 70,000 on the Madrid front.

14. "6 Meses de Guerra," *Milicia popular: Diario del 5 Regimiento del milicia popular* (Madrid), January 1937. See also Antonio Machado, "El Quinto Regimiento del 19 de Julio," *Nuestro ejército,* ano 1, no. 4 (Julio 1938), p. 10. One of the organizers of the 5th Regiment was "Carlos Contreras" or "Commandante Carlos" whose real name was Vittorio Vidali. According to *The Volunteer for Liberty,* Contreras at one time worked in a Detroit automobile factory and was also editor of a Chicago "workers' paper." But he was more than that. Under the alias of "Enea Sormenti" he served for a time as head of the Italian Bureau of the Workers Party (i.e. the Communist Party) and was deported in 1926. Another prominent Italian Communist working actively in Spain at this time in collaboration with the Spanish Communist Party was Ettore Quagliermi who went under the alias of "Pablo Clavego." An Argentine, Antonio Codovilla, went under the alias of "Medina." After the war Contreras told Bolloten that several foreigners had joined the 5th Regiment shortly after it was organized. See Longo, *Brigate,* pp. 16-19, and Bolloten, Chapter 21.

15. As early as July 26, 1936, *Mundo Obrero* printed pictures of priests allegedly captured in nonclerical attire.

16. An excellent critique of the diplomatic maneuverings at this

juncture, including the circumstances attendant to German and Italian intervention and the dilemma faced by French Premier Leon Blum, is that of Robert A. Friedlander, "Great Power Politics and Spain's Civil War: The First Phase," *The Historian,* November 1965, pp. 72-95. See also P. A. M. Van Der Esch, *Prelude to War* (The Hague, 1951) with bibliography.

17. On August 14, the German Consul in rebel-held Seville cabled the German Foreign Ministry that German pilots flying in planes and supplies did not bother to conceal their identity and were easily recognizable in their uniforms (United States, Department of State, *Documents on German Foreign Policy, 1918-1945,* Series D., Vol. III, "Germany and the Spanish Civil War, 1936-1939"—Washington, D.C., 1950—pp. 1, 38; hereafter cited as *German Documents*).

18. Pierre Cot, *Triumph of Treason* (New York, 1944), p. 341. Cot was Minister of Air in the Popular Front government of Leon Blum. Eventually some 15,000 Germans (most of them in the Condor Legion) and upwards of 50,000 Italian "volunteers" were to serve the Nationalist cause in regular military units and as technicians and advisers. Some observers, including Friedlander and Antonio Tovar (former Undersecretary for Press and Propaganda in Franco Spain and Rector of the University of Salamanca), place Italian participation at closer to 100,000 than 50,000 (Letter from Friedlander to the writer, June 1966).

19. Robert Colodny, himself a former volunteer, pointed this out in his 1950 doctoral dissertation (Berkeley, University of California), subsequently published under the title *The Struggle for Madrid: The Central Epic of the Spanish Conflict (1936-1937)* (New York, 1958).

20. Spanish Information Office, *The International Brigades: Foreign Assistants of the Spanish Reds* (Madrid, 1948), p. 17. See also *Épopée d'Espagne: Brigades internationales 1936-1939* (Paris, 1957), p. 47, and William Rust, *Britons in Spain* (London, 1939), p. 4. Rust was Communist Party organizer for Lancashire and correspondent of the London *Daily Worker.*

21. *The New York Times,* August 11, 1936, p. 2.

22. "In Memory of the Fallen Fighters of the International Brigade in Spain," *The Communist International,* vol. 4, no. 10 (October 1937), p. 747. See also *Épopée,* p. 119.

23. André Marty, "Los voluntarios de la libertad," *Nuestro ejército,* July 1938, p. 26. Wintringham (p. 37) claims that the early French volunteers were quite wary of publicity and made a point of being seen as little as possible.

24. A Swiss volunteer believes that this was the very first unit of international combatants. In response to an invitation sent by telegram, the Gastone Sozzi joined the 5th Regiment in Madrid early in September. See Max Wullschleger, *Schweizer kämpfen in Spanien: Erlebnisse der schweizer Freiwilligen in Spanien* (Zurich, 1939), pp. 21, 27. Also early in September, French volunteers who fought at Irun left after the fall of that city and went to Madrid, where, at the Montaña barracks, they reconstituted a Commune de Paris Battalion under the command of Lt. Col. J. Dumont (*Épopée,* p. 48).

25. Randolfo Pacciardi, *Il battaliogne garibaldi* (Rome, 1945), pp. 13-15.

26. Wintringham, pp. 34-36. See also Frank Jellinek, *The Civil War in Spain* (London, 1938), p. 439, and Peter Merin, pp. 298-99.

27. "Nuestros voluntarios internacionales: Por qué han venido y por qué se fueron," *Nuestro ejército,* December 1938, p. 41.

28. [XI International Brigade,] *Der österreichische Freiwillige* (Madrid, 1938), p. 33.

29. References to Americans occasionally crop up in foreign accounts of the early days of the war. Wullschleger (pp. 28, 33) claims that the one American in the Gastone Sozzi Centuria was killed on the Tardienta front. Wintringham (pp. 37-38) refers to "stop-gap" gangs of American and English pilots with "little political knowledge" who joined an air squadron organized by André Malraux: "That its headquarters, and to some extent its living quarters, happened for some time to be a Madrid hotel used by the capital's most elegant prostitutes as their quarters also was not the least of its troubles. . . . But could those boys fly!"

30. "The First Volunteer," *The Volunteer for Liberty,* May 1,

159

1938, p. 12. A few women volunteers of various nationalities were associated with the various *centuriae* in one capacity or another. See "Kathe Hempel," Wullschleger, pp. 79-86.

31. Rust, pp. 20-21. Esmond Romilly, *Boadilla* (London, 1937), p. 59. Nineteen years old at the time he went to Spain, Romilly reputedly was a nephew of Winston Churchill. Later married to Jessica Mitford (who wrote *The American Way of Death*), he was killed while serving in the R.A.F. during World War II.

32. Nick Gillain, *Le mercenaire* (Paris, 1938), p. 10. Wullschleger, pp. 22-24.

CHAPTER 2

1. Geoffrey Cox, *Defence of Madrid* (London, 1937), p. 163.
2. Born in 1899, Pacciardi received a degree in law at the University of Rome in 1921. He joined the Italian Republican Party in 1919 and was imprisoned shortly after Mussolini's rise to power. He escaped to Switzerland only to be expelled to France.
3. Luigi Gallo, *Un anno di guèrra in Spagna* (Paris, 1938), p. 152; and *Brigate internazionali*, p. 18.
4. Pacciardi, *Il battaglione garibaldi* (Rome, 1945), pp. 17-40.
5. *International Press Correspondence,* August 1, 1936, p. 950.
6. *Foreign Relations of the United States* (Washington, D.C., continuing series), 1938, II, 461.
7. Pierre Broué and Émile Témime, *La révolution et la guerre d'Espagne* (Paris, 1961), p. 339. But this source should be used with a great deal of caution. The authors assert (p. 347, n. 11) that General Pyotr N. Wrangel, the last White commander in the Crimea, served with the Loyalist forces under the orders of a former adversary, General "Walter," to earn his way back to Russia and was killed in action. This makes an interesting story, but Wrangel died in Brussels in 1928.
8. Hugh Thomas, *The Spanish Civil War* (New York, 1961), p. 216. The propaganda campaign was foreshadowed by Stalin's telegram of October 16 to the Spanish Communist

Party in which he declared the liberation of Spain from fascism to be "the concern of all advanced and progressive humanity."

9. See also Stalin's later statement, Part vii of "The Foundations of Leninism" in *Works* (Moscow, 1953), vol. 6, p. 161.

10. Certain other sources—Luis Maria de Lojendio, *Operaciones militares de la guerra de España, 1936-1939* (Barcelona, 1940), pp. 177-78; Office of Spanish Information, *The International Brigades: Foreign Assistants of the Spanish Reds* (Madrid, 1948), pp. 57-60; and Walter G. Krivitsky, *In Stalin's Secret Service* (New York, 1939), pp. 75-115—give accounts of a trip to Moscow by Maurice Thorez, the French Communist leader, to plead the Loyalist cause with Georgi Dimitrov, Secretary General of the Comintern, and of a Politburo meeting at which the decision to intervene was taken. But none of the authors can have had any documentary evidence or first-hand knowledge of such high-level negotiations or decisions in Moscow. Krivitsky, a Soviet defector who was important (or loquacious?) enough to be murdered in Washington in 1941, gives the most plausible account. He claims to have been the chief of Red Army intelligence in Western Europe, but Alexander Orlov, the N.K.G.B. chief in Spain who was in a position to know, says Krivitsky was merely the resident N.K.G.B. agent in the Netherlands.

11. Louis Fischer, *Men and Politics* (New York, 1941), pp. 377, 382. *German Documents,* p. 89.

12. The Nationalists later captured a few Soviet merchant seamen, some of whom were eventually exchanged for German citizens imprisoned in Russia, but apparently they never took any Russian military prisoners—hardly surprising since Stalin had warned his military advisers and technicians to "stay out of range of the artillery fire!"

And just who were these "advisers"? Luis Araquistain avers that shortly after Largo Caballero became Premier (September 4), Soviet Ambassador Marcel Rosenberg introduced a General "Goriev" to the Spanish Government, identifying him as military attaché and offering his services. According to Alvarez del Vayo, early in September Rosenberg introduced a certain

"Major Ramler" of the Soviet General Staff to Finance Minister Negrín, while the Soviet military attaché was known as General "Grigorovitch." Krivitsky claims that the Soviet military staff and personnel were headed by a General "Berzin," that they never numbered more than 2,000, and that they were ceaselessly watched by the N.K.G.B., who endeavored to keep their presence a secret. Correspondent Herbert Matthews refers to a General "de Gorieff" (whose real name he believed to be "Van Rosen") and agrees with Krivitsky that the Soviet officers were kept under cover: "none of us saw or knew anything in particular about them." On the other hand, Louis Fischer, who was in Madrid in September, refers to a General "Grishin" as the ranking Soviet officer (at least before the summer of 1938), although he says he never met Grishin and claims that General Goriev, the "military attaché," was the guiding hand in the defense of Madrid. Fischer also says that he was struck by the complete lack of effort to conceal the presence of the Soviet officers, Goriev in particular. Colodny offers the rather convincing conclusion that "Goriev," "Grishin," "Grigorovitch," said "Berzin" were one and the same. As he points out, Krivitsky never mentions "Goriev," while other writers and observers (Fischer, for example) never mention "Berzin" or, alternatively, "Grigorovitch."

The Soviet press correspondent Michael Kol'tsov also exercised a great deal of influence in Madrid during the first part of the war. Colodny claims that his *Ispanskiy Dnevnik* [Spanish Diary] (Moscow, 1957) "reflects not only the mind of a veteran Bolshevik, but also considerable military training." He also mentions Kol'tsov's hourly telephone calls to Moscow during the heavy fighting for Madrid. Arturo Barea, who worked in the censorship bureau in the War Ministry, comments that Kol'tsov "intervened in most of the discussions on the authority of his vitality and arrogant will." On one occasion Kol'tsov personally threatened him with a court martial but backed down on the orders of his own superiors, "whoever they were."

Finally, Dolores Ibarruri in her memoirs claims that a

162

number of officers who later rose to high rank in World War II also served in Spain, among them Marshal Rodion Ya. Malinovsky, Khrushchev's Defense Minister. For obvious reasons, Soviet propagandists have never denied this and similar stories. But, as Khrushchev mentioned in his "secret" speech of 1956, "the cadre of leaders who had gained military experience in Spain and in the Far East was almost completely liquidated." And the Soviet journalist Ilya Ehrenburg, attempting to atone for his services to Stalin by telling the truth, admits that practically all those who served in Spain were later shot. At least one other did survive, however—Alexander Orlov, the N.K.G.B. chief, who defected when ordered to return home.

For the various accounts of Soviet personnel in Madrid, see Colonel Segismundo Casado, *The Last Days of Madrid* (London, 1939), pp. 51-52; Luis Araquistain, *El communismo y la guerra de España* (Carmaux, France, 1939), p. 24; Alvarez del Vayo, *The Last Optimist* (New York, 1950), pp. 290-91; Krivitsky, p. 95; Herbert Matthews, *Two Wars and More to Come* (New York, 1938), pp. 212-13; Fischer, *Men and Politics,* pp. 395, 412; Adolfo Lizon-Gadea, *Brigadas internacionales en España* (Madrid, 1940), p. 79; "Wayfarer," *The International Brigade* (Hassocks, 1939?), p. 6; Colodny, pp. 162-65, n. 100; Arturo Barea, *The Clash* (London, 1944), pp. 175, 194; Dolores Ibarruri, *El único camino* (Mexico, D.F., 1963), pp. 314-15.

13. Gustav Regler, *The Owl of Minerva* (New York, 1959), p. 276. At the time a Communist, Regler soon became Political Commissar of the XII [International] Brigade.

14. Longo makes no reference to Togliatti, but according to Gates, Togliatti was the envoy of the Comintern to the Politburo of the Spanish Communist Party, and "as such, he was the most powerful Communist figure in Spain." He reportedly went under the name of "Alfredo," and while he did not appear in public, as did both Marty and Longo, "his responsibility was the whole policy of the Spanish Communists, and not merely the International Brigades." Gates attributes the enormous growth of the Spanish Communist Party after the revolt

163

largely to Togliatti's advice and leadership. One of the principal authors of the Popular-Front policy, "Togliatti was a brilliant tactician, probably the most capable in the Communist world." (Comments to the writer, May 1966.)

15. Nor did all of the volunteers arrive by foot, train, boat, or bus. One Dutch volunteer, at least, managed to travel in style, flying from Toulouse to Barcelona via Air France. Johan Brouwer, *In den Schaduw van den Dood* (Zutphen, n.d.,), pp. 23-30.

16. *Épopée,* p. 50.

17. *Épopée,* p. 51, claims that Martínez Barrio asked just what conditions the delegation attached to their offer, to which they replied, "None," that their only desire was to have the International Brigades subordinated to the authority of the Spanish Government and military command and used as shock troops whenever necessary.

18. Longo, *Brigate internazionali,* pp. 30-31, 37-44. In the meantime, on October 10, Stalin had prepared the way for public disclosure of the action already decided upon: The Soviet representative in the London Nonintervention Committee declared that, if the repeated violations of the Nonintervention Accord by Germany, Italy, and Portugal did not cease forthwith, his government would consider itself free from any obligations assumed under the terms of the Agreement (see *The New York Times,* October 12, 1936). And on October 23, the Soviet representative informed the London Committee that the Nonintervention Agreement had turned out to be "an empty, torn scrap of paper," and his government would restore to the Spanish Government their legal right under international law to purchase arms. (Alvarez del Vayo, *Freedom's Battle,* pp. 75-76.)

CHAPTER 3

1. For a detailed account of this phase of the war see Colodny, Chapter 3: "The Road from Toledo." Also Luis María de Lojendio, *Operaciones militares de la guerra de España 1936-*

1939 (Barcelona, 1940), pp. 160-76, and Harold G. Cardozo, *The March of a Nation* (London, 1937), Chapter 7. Cardozo was a reporter for the *Daily Mail* assigned to the rebel forces.

2. At the time of his first visit to Madrid early in September, Pacciardi (pp. 17-18) observed that "Caballero has strange ideas about modern war." In response to a query regarding the absence of trenches and defensive preparations, the Prime Minister asked how the militiamen could possibly advance if at the same time they were digging trenches.

3. *The Economist,* October 10, 1936, p. 62.

4. Julián Zugazagoitia, *Historia de la guerra de España* (Buenos Aires, 1940), pp. 162, 181-83. See also General Vicente Rojo, *España Heroica* (Buenos Aires, 1942); and Colodny, pp. 43-46, 171 n. 27.

5. Manuel Aznar, *Historia militar de la guerra de España (1936-1939)* (Madrid, 1940), p. 277; Lojendio, p. 170; Colodny, pp. 34, 36, 48.

6. "The Development of the Peoples' Army," *The Volunteer for Liberty,* June 8, 1937, p. 4. Miaja's orders to the field commanders were to retreat "only to the cemetery" (Zugazagoitia, p. 183).

7. Born in 1889, André Marty's career as a revolutionary began in 1918. A sailor on a French warship in the Black Sea sent to threaten the Bolsheviks holding Odessa, Marty organized a group of sailors and delivered an ultimatum to the fleet commander: withdraw and return to France or have the ship sailed home by the mutineers. The French units withdrew, but Marty drew a twenty-year prison sentence for his efforts. Released in response to popular clamor after four and a half years in a military prison, he was first elected to the Chamber of Deputies in 1924.

8. Pacciardi, *Il battaglione garibaldi,* pp. 41-45. The committee at Albacete confirmed Pacciardi as commander of the Garibaldi Battalion, although not to have done so might have jeopardized the much emphasized unity of the various antifascist elements. Longo claims (*Brigate,* p. 70) that Pacciardi's appointment merely proved that "we" (the Communists) didn't intend to take advantage of the "Communist majority"

to stack all positions of command with Party membership. And Gates referred "to Togliatti's long-standing policy to promote broad anti-fascist unity as the best means of strengthening the Communist Party" (memorandum to the writer, May 1966).

9. *Las brigadas internacionales según testimonio de sus artífices* (Barcelona [1939?]), p. 79; *L'Humanité,* October 18, 1937. Longo *(Brigate,* p. 69) claims that by October 22 between 3,000 and 4,000 volunteers had arrived at Albacete.

10. Francisco Franco y Bahamonde, *Speech Delivered by the Head of the State* (Madrid, 1949), p. 3.

11. In most armies, only army corps are numbered with Roman numerals. Most of the contemporary accounts and subsequent literature, however, have used Roman numerals in references to the International Brigades, and the practice has been followed in the present work in order to distinguish the Internationals from Spanish units.

12. Longo *(Brigate,* pp. 68-70) claims the appeal came directly from the Spanish Communist Party, but Colodny believes the order may have come from General "Goriev." See also *Épopée,* p. 51; Rust, p. 16; Pacciardi, p. 59; *International Press Correspondence,* October 23, 1937; *Épopée* (p. 75) asserts that the Edgar André Battalion left Albacete for the front on October 28. And a German officer of the Edgar André claims that the XI Brigade went into battle with only 1,700 effectives—Gustav Szinda, *Die XI Brigade* (Berlin, 1956), pp. 10-24. The precise number of volunteers in the first International Brigade (and in the other brigades as well) may never be known, simply because very little was kept in the way of records. By Longo's own admission (p. 175), the early volunteers went into combat without any official identification.

13. Fischer says that he enlisted two days after the siege of Madrid began, and that "I am as proud of that as I am of anything I have done in my life" *(Men and Politics,* p. 386).

14. *Ibid.,* pp. 387-89.

15. "On November 7th at 8 P.M. the 12th Brigade . . . left the base for Madrid." André Marty, "The International Brigades

—Twelve Magnificent Months" (Part II), *International Press Correspondence,* October 30, 1937, p. 1044. But Longo claims that the XII didn't leave Albacete until November 10.

16. Romilly, pp. 61, 74. Romilly says he was first invited to join nine English fellows of the Tom Mann Centuria who in turn voted [sic] to join the Thälmanns. See also Peter Kerrigan, "The First British Company," *The Volunteer for Liberty,* August 13, 1938, pp. 4-5. Apparently a few English volunteers also served in the Franco-Belge Battalion.

17. Zugazagoitia, p. 186; Colodny, pp. 56-63. Originally scheduled for November 7, the attack apparently was postponed because of delays encountered by some of the rebel units. The Republicans had expected an attack around the southern perimeter of Madrid towards Vallecas in an attempt to cut the capital off from Valencia. For this reason the XI Brigade had originally been dispatched to Vallecas rather than directly to Madrid.

18. An interesting account of the fifth column and the experiences of rebel sympathizers in Madrid is that of Augustin Foxá, *Madrid: De corte a cheka* (San Sebastian, 1938). For another interesting personal narrative, of an American girl sympathetic to the Loyalists, see Janet Risenfeld, *Dancer in Madrid* (New York, 1938).

19. Henry Buckley, *Life and Death of the Spanish Republic* (London, 1940), pp. 262-63.

20. *The New York Times,* November 6, 1936, p. 1.

21. Geoffrey Cox, pp. 66-67. Herbert Matthews (*Two Wars and More to Come,* pp. 208-9) and Fischer (*Men and Politics,* p. 393) state that the Spanish militiamen long regarded the Internationals as Russians.

22. John Sommerfield, *Volunteer in Spain* (New York, 1937), pp. 84-85.

23. Cardozo (p. 180) claims that rebels crossed the Manzanares on November 7 and penetrated as far as the Plaza de España, only to be driven back. Colodny (pp. 65-68) claims that early on November 8 Moroccan troops crossed the Manzanares below the West Park, only to be wiped out, and that shortly after noon, elements of the rebel columns of Colonels Asensio and

Castejón first yielded ground to the Internationals in the Casa de Campo. Geoffrey Cox indicates that the Poles of the Dombrowsky Battalion repelled a rebel attack at Villaverde on the night of the 8th; but *Épopée* (pp. 78-79) claims that the second company of the Commune de Paris first came under fire when it was surprised by a rebel patrol in the Casa de Campo on November 9. The company reportedly lost two sections in this initial engagement. The German Szinda also says that the XI Brigade first saw action on the 9th, the day after the "fascists" reached Frenchman's Bridge and crossed the Manzanares, while Longo (*Brigate,* p. 73) states that it was on the 9th that the Commune and Dombrowsky fought with the enemy at the approaches to the University City. He also asserts that it was on the night of the 9th that the Edgar André attacked and recaptured Frenchman's Bridge. Much of the discrepancy in these various accounts may be due to the rapidity with which events transpired during the first twenty-four hours following the arrival of the Internationals. Thus, Cox states that on the 9th the whole XI Brigade was concentrated in the University City sector, from which General Kleber then launched it in the first attack into the Casa de Campo.

24. Longo (*Brigate,* p. 85) recalled "the terrible organization deficiency of our improvised brigade" and admits that he and General Lukacz spent one whole night on the battlefield looking for command posts—"not always with success." Food and other supplies also failed to arrive.

25. Again there is a rather wide range of views as to just when the XII Brigade actually arrived in Madrid. Fischer (p. 393) says it was November 14, but Pacciardi (p. 74) says the 16th, and Longo (p. 88) the 17th.

26. Longo, *Brigate,* pp. 94-99; Pacciardi, pp. 73-83; Colodny, pp. 70-82. Colodny states that Miaja blundered in allowing the Anarchist column of Buenaventura Durruti to deploy in the Casa de Campo when it arrived from Barcelona on November 14. Directly in Varela's path, the C.N.T. troops broke under the onslaught. Subsequently the Anarchists fought very well in the University City where Durruti was killed—according to

rumors, shot in the back. See A. G. Gilbert, *Durruti, un anarchista integro* (Barcelona, 1937?).

27. Fischer, *Men and Politics,* p. 394; Cox, p. 144. After November 15, the Loyalists, in addition to the two International Brigades, had elements of the 5th Regiment, and the Ortega, Durruti, Tierra y Libertad, Mera, Perea, and Cavada columns defending the city—Rojo, *Alerta Los Pueblos!* (Buenos Aires, 1939), p. 55. Longo (*Brigate,* p. 116) says the defensive forces consisted of seven to ten thousand members of the 5th Regiment, "a few thousand" militia connected with Socialist and Republican organizations, some seven or eight thousand members of the C.N.T., and the two International Brigades.

28. Cardozo, p. 194.

29. Detailed accounts of the fighting from the Nationalist side may be found in Lojendio, Cardozo, and Aznar. On the Republican side excellent personal narratives are those of Pacciardi, Romilly, Sommerfield, Wintringham, and Regler (both *The Great Crusade* and *The Owl of Minerva*), as well as those of Lise Lindbaeck (*Internationaella brigaden*—Stockholm, 1939) and, to a certain extent, Wullschleger. Rojo's *España Heroica,* Longo's *Brigate internazionali,* and Theodore Balk's *La quatorzième* (Madrid, 1937) are also valuable. Colodny gives analysis as well as description (Chapter 2), while Hugh Thomas provides pretty full coverage in his Chapters 41-43.

30. Pacciardi, pp. 85-95. Significantly, Longo does not mention Pacciardi's citation. Nenni, *La guerre d'Espagne* (Paris, 1960), pp. 169-70, on the other hand, credits Pacciardi with having held the greatest confidence of his troops from the very outset.

31. Longo, *Brigate,* p. 117. This was the first of many such shifts that were to take place in the International Brigades during the course of the war. Longo continually refers to the Franco-Belge Battalion rather than to the André Marty, apparently to avoid mentioning one who subsequently fell from grace in the eyes of the Party.

32. Romilly, pp. 283-84; Pacciardi, pp. 103-8. Cardozo (p. 230) visited Boadilla shortly after the town fell to the rebels and observed that "the Reds were lying in great numbers all over

169

the place. In many cases they had held their ground despite shelling and machine gunning, and the trenches were only captured after hand-to-hand fighting in which hand grenades and the bayonet had been used . . . [But] hand-to-hand fighting entails losses on either side, and it was certain that the Nationalist attacking columns must have paid a heavy price."

33. Pacciardi, pp. 113-26; Longo, *Brigate,* pp. 183-87.

34. Longo, *Brigate,* p. 194-97; Lindbaeck, p. 90; *Épopée,* p. 92; Wullschleger, pp. 118-26.

35. Theodore Balk, pp. 91-106. In the course of what has been dubbed "The Battle in the Mist," one battalion of the XIV Brigade got lost and never returned. This may have been the ill-fated 9th Battalion, which previously suffered a calamity in its very first operation in southern Spain (discussed in the next chapter) and whose history, according to Balk, "closed" at Las Rozas. See also Wullschleger, pp. 118-26, and Colodny, p. 104.

36. Regler, *The Great Crusade* (novel—New York, 1940), pp. 216-17, 221-22.

37. See "International Brigades in University City," *Life,* December 28, 1936, p. 58.

38. Szinda, p. 30. The 600 survivors plus the 1,230 casualties gives a figure very close to the 1,900 estimated as the original strength of the Brigade. Longo (*Brigate,* p. 208) states that to an original strength of "about 2,000" the Brigade received an additional 1,000 replacements prior to its period of rest at Murcia, at which time it counted about 1,000 effectives. This would imply that the Brigade suffered some 2,000 casualties. But any such assessment is complicated by the shift of the Thälmann from the XII to the XI Brigade and of the Dombrowsky from the XI to the XII, which took place during this period. See also F. Dahlem, "The Military-Political Work of the Eleventh International Brigade," *The Communist International,* May 1938, p. 447.

39. While in Murcia, the XI Brigade apparently incorporated a number of Spanish recruits into its three battalions, and in addition "organized" two new battalions composed entirely of Spaniards. Longo asserts that one of these, created from an

Anarchist unit, "caused the Brigade every sort of difficulty" and refused to go to the front when ordered on the "pretext" of not having received any arms. The XII Brigade reportedly drew Spanish replacements from the Madrid and Prieto battalions. (Longo, *Brigate,* pp. 212-13).

40. For example, Fischer, *Men and Politics,* p. 393; Zugazagoitia, pp. 195-96; and Regler, *Owl of Minerva,* p. 283, say the brigades did save Madrid. But "Don't let us exaggerate: our Brigade did not save Madrid," declared Wintringham (pp. 135-36). "Madrid would have saved itself without us. But without us Franco would have got further into Madrid." Nenni (pp. 193, 242) and Dolores Ibarruri (*El único camino,* pp. 309, 314) agree that the brigades were only one of several important factors.

41. Manual Aznar (pp. 282, 325) credits the Internationals with great "spirit, courage and faith."

42. *The International Brigades,* p. 81.

43. Quoted by Geoffrey Cox, pp. 188-89. As to the broader issue of propaganda, Arturo Barea (pp. 189, 195) states that shortly after the XI Brigade first appeared in Madrid, Gustav Regler asked him to give more publicity to the Internationals. And "after a week or so it appeared . . . as though they were the sole saviours of Madrid . . . I was angry, because I found it unjust that the people of Madrid, the improvised soldiers . . . were forgotten because there was no propaganda machine to show them up."

44. Fischer, *Men and Politics,* p. 398; Rojo *Alerta los pueblos!,* pp. 50-52.

45. Frank Pitcairn, "The International Brigade," *The World Review,* January 1937, p. 43.

46. Krivitsky, "Stalin's Hand in Spain," *Saturday Evening Post,* April 15, 1939, p. 118.

47. "Matei Zalka," *The Communist International,* September 1937, pp. 656-58.

48. Regler, *Owl of Minerva,* p. 283; Herbert Matthews, *The Education of a Correspondent* (New York, 1946), p. 143-44. Antonio López Fernández, *Defensa de Madrid* (Mexico City, 1945), pp. 83-84; Bolloten, p. 237 n. 50.

CHAPTER 4

1. Longo, *Brigate,* p. 137. See also Wullschleger, p. 177, 180, 195; and *Épopée,* p. 52.
2. Alfred Kantorowicz, *Tschapaiew: Das Battalion der 21 Nationen* (Rudolstadt, 1952), pp. 16-17, 25. See also Wullschleger, p. 108; and Longo, *Brigate,* p. 138. The 11th Battalion may have been called the "Mickiewicz" and the 7th the "Louise Michel" (*Épopée,* p. 249).
3. Kantorowicz, pp. 9-10.
4. Balk, pp. 40-45, 48-65; *Épopée,* p. 52, 87; Nick Gillain, *Le mercenaire* (Paris, 1938), p. 27. Together with Longo's *Brigate* these are the most informative works on the XIV Brigade, about which there is otherwise very little information. Balk's *Quatorzième,* like Kantorowicz' *Tschapaiew,* only covers the period from November 1936 to August 1937. See also Rust, pp. 26-27; Peter Kerrigan, "The First British Company," *The Volunteer for Liberty,* August 13, 1938, pp. 4-5; and *General Karol Swierczewski* (Warsaw, 1950).
5. *Le livre de la 15ème brigade internationale: Nos combats contre le fascisme* (Madrid, 1937), p. 15; Carlo Penchienati, *Brigate internazionali in Spagna* (Milan, 1950), pp. 20-22; "Copic, Commander of our 15th Brigade," *The Volunteer for Liberty,* November 17, 1937, p. 4.
6. Edwin Rolfe, *The Lincoln Battalion* (New York, 1939), pp. 6, 9, 18-24, 71. See also "American Volunteers in Spain," *The Volunteer for Liberty,* November 7, 1938, p. 9. Rolfe states that 2,800 Americans served in Spain and that "perhaps 1,800" returned to the United States, thus implying losses of about 1,000. Gates concurs in the figure of 1,000 killed as the most credible estimate, the figure given immediately after the war. With the passage of time, the tendency has been to exaggerate the number of the dead. Although most Americans served as shock troops, many were in medical, transport, artillery and other units that suffered fewer casualties. (Memorandum to the writer, May 1966.)

7. Sandor Voros, *American Commissar* (New York, 1961), pp. 333, 348; Gates, memorandum to the writer, May 1966; Longo, *Brigate,* p. 213; Rolfe, p. 19.

8. Robert Hale Merriman was twenty-eight at the time. His father was a lumberjack and his mother a writer. He had worked his way through the University of Nevada, majored in economics, and was a member of the football team and R.O.T.C. He won a fellowship at the University of California, where he taught as a graduate student, and went to Europe in 1936 to study agricultural problems. Fischer claims that Merriman, a tennis partner of former years, was in Moscow in January 1937, and called him one afternoon to inquire about getting to Spain. (*Men and Politics,* p. 403; see also *Among Friends*—New York, Spring 1938—p. 2; and Rolfe, pp. 9-10.) Sandor Voros claims that Merriman told him that he did not join the Party because he considered it much too confining. Voros (pp. 344-48) also states that Merriman told him he came to Spain because, when he was in Moscow, he had been made to feel "ashamed" that no American had yet enlisted in the International Brigades. Significantly, Communist sources do not indicate that Merriman was a Party member, and in 1955 the Subversive Activities Control Board, in its *Report and Order* (p. 16) on the Veterans of the Abraham Lincoln Brigade, concluded that Merriman was not, in fact, a Party functionary.

9. Rolfe, pp. 3-4.

10. Longo, *Brigate,* pp. 139-43; Colodny, pp. 94, 208 n. 13; Kantorowicz, pp. 23-27.

11. André Marty, "The International Brigades," *International Press Correspondence,* May 17, 1938, p. 585. Longo, *Brigate,* pp. 145-46.

12. For an interesting account of "The Last Days of Málaga," see Arthur Koestler, *Spanish Testament* (London, 1937), pp. 178-204.

13. Kantorowicz, pp. 48-49, 62-65. Longo (p. 320) says that "the atmosphere" in this region was not as "heroic and enthusiastic as at Madrid" and that the Internationals didn't find it at all easy to overcome "prejudice and preconceived hostility."

14. John Gates, *The Story of an American Communist* (New

York, 1958), p. 49; Longo, *Brigate,* pp. 326-27. In April the XIII Brigade or some of its units may have been used against the rebel redoubt of La Virgen (or Nuestra Señora) de la Cabeza, a sanctuary high in the mountains of the Sierra Morena some 20 kilometers from Andujar, behind the front lines. *The Volunteer for Liberty* of June 1, 1937 does carry a picture with the caption, "Peasants were shut up as hostages in La Virgen de la Cabeza. Here they are seen talking with their liberators." The uniforms of the soldiers appear to be those of Internationals, but they are not identified, and there is no other commentary accompanying the picture.

15. Longo, *Brigate,* pp. 148-53. See also *Épopée,* p. 249, and Wullschleger, p. 118.

16. Balk, pp. 126-27, 169. Actually, the two battalions may have been merged. An entirely new name eventually was adopted by the 10th Battalion, however.

17. A. Donaldson, "Britains in Spain," *The Volunteer for Liberty,* September 20, 1937, p. 3.

18. Casado, p. 64; Rojo, *España heroica,* pp. 63-69; Lojendio, pp. 195-200; and Colodny, pp. 110-12. The rebel offensive apparently was designed to coincide with the attack on Málaga, and, according to Colodny, actually was planned by the German generals Sperrle, von Faupel, and von Thoma. Wintringham's *English Captain* is concerned primarily with the Jarama campaign and, together with Colodny's *The Struggle for Madrid,* is one of the more informative works.

19. Casado, pp. 64-65, 67. The result, according to Casado, was to help the Communists gain control of the Army of the Center, because Miaja was their favorite. By his own admission, Casado, who was not particularly fond of Miaja and loathed the Communists, was responsible for resolving the Pozas-Miaja tiff in favor of the latter. The Loyalist forces at Jarama were subsequently organized as the III Army Corps consisting of Division A: 5th, XII, XIV Brigades (Lt. Col. Arce); Division B: XI, XV, 17th Brigades (General Gall); Division C: 16th, 19th, 24th Brigades (Lt. Col. Rubert); and Division 11: 1st, 18th, 23rd Brigades (Lt. Col. Lister)—Rojo, *España,* pp. 70-71.

20. Balk, pp. 113-14; Regler, *The Great Crusade,* pp. 260-61, and

The Owl of Minerva, p. 287; Colodny, pp. 118-19; Longo, *Brigate,* pp. 228-30; Lojendio, p. 200; Pacciardi, pp. 160-62; Nenni, pp. 173-74. Regler, an eyewitness, comments: "They were a battalion much given to complaining, who had sometimes seemed to me to be thoroughly demoralized," but when the chips were down they "forgot their grievances and anarchist self-righteousness" and fought extremely well.

21. Quoted by Rust, p. 52; see also Buckley, p. 287.
22. Balk, pp. 115-17; *Épopée,* pp. 97-98; Colodny, p. 226, n. 137; Szinda, pp. 40-45; Rolfe, p. 33; Longo, pp. 230-31. According to Longo, the Republicans used anti-aircraft cannon for the very first time during the Jarama fighting. The Loyalist air force, including the Malraux squadron, also was effective.
23. Quoted by Rolfe, pp. 49-50.
24. Roberto Catalupo (Italian Ambassador to Nationalist Spain), *Fu la Spagna* (Milan, 1948), pp. 196-97; Wintringham, p. 182.
25. Rolfe, pp. 55-57; Wintringham, pp. 257-58; Hemingway's preface to Regler's *Great Crusade,* p. vii; Matthews, *Two Wars and More to Come,* pp. 222-23.
26. Colodny (p. 229, n. 158) gives the following casualty figures for the Internationals (dead, wounded, and missing):

	Pre-Battle Effectives	Casualties
XI Brigade	1,500	1,200
Thälmann	500	450
Edgar André	500	300
Commune de Paris	500	450
XII Brigade	3,000	1,700
Garibaldi	1,000	500
Dombrowsky	1,000	600
André Marty	1,000	600
XV Brigade	2,700	2,250
British	600	500
Dimitrov	800	700
6th February	800	700
Lincoln	500	350
XIV Brigade	1,500	400
	8,700	5,550

Penchienati (pp. 22-23) states that the Dimitrov lost about 450 of the battalion's original strength of 780-800 men, and Longo (pp. 237-38) claims that each of the International Brigades went into battle with 2,000-2,500 effectives and averaged casualties well in excess of 50 per cent.

27. Aznar, pp. 363-68. Aznar claims that the battle was a success for the Nationalists, "but not a complete success," while Werner Beumelberg, historian of the Condor Legion, considers the battle a victory for the Republicans, which he attributes to "the Russian tanks, the International Brigades and the excellence of their flying units"—*Kampf um Spanien* (Berlin, 1939), p. 74.

28. F. Dahlem, "The Military-Political Work of the Eleventh International Brigade," *The Communist International,* May 1938, p. 448. As for the morale of the troops left at the Jarama, Longo (pp. 249, 325) asserts that "only the arrival of mail was able, just for an instant, to shake off the general lethargy and awaken some sense of hope, only to be followed by even greater despair." In addition, "many volunteers took advantage of the first moments of calm along the front to undertake an [unauthorized] escapade in the capital."

29. In addition to the four Italian divisions the Nationalist forces consisted of the Spanish Soria Division under General Moscardo, Carlist Requetes, and elements of the Tercio (Aznar, p. 378; and Lojendio, p. 210). The Loyalist forces were quickly organized into the V Army Corps, consisting of the 11th (Lister) Division, with the 1st, 46th, and 42nd Spanish Brigades and the XI Brigade; the 14th (Mera) Division, with the 65th, 70th, and XII Brigades; and the 12th Division composed of three Spanish brigades. Two other Spanish brigades were brought up from Madrid into flank and reserve positions. (Rojo, *España,* p. 85; Colodny, p. 135; Longo, *Brigate,* p. 276.)

30. Regler says that the leaflet-laden Garibaldis "felt like the herald angels at Christmas, but they would not talk and sing, since the shepherds on the other side would certainly answer them with rifle fire." But some of the volunteers (all of them Communists, according to Regler) complained that "if the

Italians on the other side are so ready to desert, why aren't they shooting their officers? We aren't the Salvation Army." Regler claims that Anelito Barontini, the Communist commander of the Garibaldi Battalion, called the loudspeaker propaganda "mass murder of the [International] volunteers with musical accompaniment," but Longo asserts that this propaganda "had a profound effect . . . naturally, each prisoner quickly makes it known that he is not a Fascist and never was." (Regler, *Great Crusade,* p. 337, *Owl of Minerva,* pp. 305, 310; Longo, *Brigate,* pp. 289, 300.)

31. Ernest Hemingway visited the scene of battle shortly after the fighting and estimated the number of Italian dead alone at between 2,000 and 3,000 (*The Spanish War*—London, 1938— pp. 8-9). Colodny (p. 237, n. 217) points out that it is impossible to establish reliable figures for the Italian casualties, but feels that an estimate of 6,000 wounded would be consistent with the figure of 3,000 killed and 2,500 prisoners cited by Lopez-Fernandez, who did have access to the files of the General Staff. On the Republican side the Edgar André Battalion of the XI Brigade was particularly hard hit, with only some 180 of its men surviving unwounded. (Dahlem, "The Military-Political Work of the Eleventh International Brigade," *The Communist International,* May 1938, p. 449; Szinda, pp. 52-54.)

32. *The Italian Invasion of Spain* (Washington, D.C., 1937), pp. 277, 309-11.

33. Rojo, *España heroica,* pp. 79, 84-85. Aznar (p. 388) admits that the Nationalists made several mistakes, including concentrating their troops in small areas and deploying their artillery too close to the front lines where it was easily spotted and hit by the Republican aircraft. Perhaps more important, General Mancini informed von Faupel, the German Ambassador to Franco Spain, that the training and composition of his units, and particularly of the officers, left much to be desired (*German Documents,* p. 269-70).

CHAPTER 5

1. José Martín Blázquez, *I Helped to Build an Army* (London, 1939), p. 296; "Our Army Is a Peoples' Army," *The Volunteer for Liberty,* June 1, 1937, p. 1; José Díaz, "Organizing the Victory of the People," *The Communist International,* March 1937, pp. 318-31; George Orwell, *Homage to Catalonia* London, 1938); Gates, memorandum.

2. This is the estimate of Gustav Regler—*The Owl of Minerva,* p. 311—but it appears consistent with figures cited by other observers.

3. Penchienati, *Brigate internazionali in Spagna,* pp. 31-33; Gates, *The Story of an American Communist,* p. 54.

4. Kantorowicz, p. 164; Szinda, pp. 10-23; International Brigades, *Der österreichische Freiwillige,* pp. 35-37; Julián Henríquez Caubín, *La Batalla del Ebro* (Mexico City, 1944), pp. 32-38— this source also identifies, by number, the battalions of the XIII and XV Brigades and with information from other quarters makes possible the identification of the units of the XII and XIV Brigades.

5. Pacciardi, *Battaglione garibaldi,* p. 204.

6. Longo, *Brigate,* p. 340; Penchienati, *Brigate internazionali in Spagna,* pp. 64-65; Pacciardi, *Battaglione garibaldi,* pp. 203-4.

7. Kantorowicz, pp. 129, 176-83; Henríquez Caubín, p. 38.

8. The title page of *La quatorzième* lists several battalions which were in the XIV Brigade up to the time of the book's publication in the summer of 1937. Included are the 9th Battalion, Domingo Germinal, Ralph Fox, Henri Barbusse, Commune de Paris, Henri Vuillemin, Pierre Brachet, and André Marty. *Épopée* (p. 248) adds the Vaillant Couturier and the "6th of February," but does not include the Ralph Fox.

9. This is indicated by the known designations of the battalions in the XI, XIII, and XV Brigades of the 35th Division.

10. Rolfe, pp. 76-77. See also "The History of the MacKenzie-Papineau Battalion," *The Volunteer for Liberty,* November 7, 1938, pp. 4-5, and "Canadians in Spain," *The Volunteer for*

Liberty, March 7, 1938, p. 4. According to the *Volunteer,* a thousand Canadians were in Spain by the end of 1937. Many of them appear to have been foreign-born rather than natives of Canada.

11. Gates, *The Story of an American Communist,* p. 57; *Le livre de la 15ème brigade internationale,* pp. 297-303.

12. Rolfe, pp. 86-88; *The Volunteer for Liberty:* "American Hospitals in Spain" (August 30, 1937, pp. 4-5), "American Hospital Unit in Action" (December 6, 1937, pp. 6-7), and "Doctor Barksy Returns to Spain" (December 13, 1937, p. 11). See also Lini Fuhr, "I was a Nurse in Loyalist Spain," *Among Friends* (New York), vol. I, no. 2 (Spring 1938), p. 10. Voros (p. 321) claims that the John Brown Battery, which consisted of some seventy or eighty Americans (half of them foreign-born) did not have any guns during most of the training period. When guns finally arrived in June 1937, most of them allegedly were given to Czechoslovak batteries.

13. In the closest thing to an "official" estimate from Communist sources, Dolores Ibarruri (La Pasionaria) mentions "35,000 authentic international volunteers, including Soviets" of whom 5,000 were killed—*Historia del partido comunista de España* (Warsaw, 1960), p. 136. This is in line with the estimate of 30,000-35,000 given by the non-Communist Carlo Penchienati (p. 54). Perhaps 10,000 of the volunteers were French, while Belgians may have numbered an additional 1,200. This guess (the writer's) is predicated upon various references to the apparently substantial proportion of Belgian volunteers in several International units during the fall of 1936. A Polish source places Polish volunteers at 4,500 (Ignacy Blum, *Z Dziejow Aparatu politycznego Wojska polskiego*—Warsaw, 1957— p. 4), but Broué and Témime point out that many of these were working as miners in France and Belgium at the time the Civil War broke out. This complicates an accurate assessment of the number of bona fide French and Belgian volunteers.

Germans and Austrians together came to approximately 5,000 (2,000 killed)—Alfred Kantorowicz, *Spanisches Tagebuch* (Berlin, 1949), p. 15. Swiss volunteers apparently amounted to 150 or so. Dutch and Scandinavians together may have totaled close to a thousand, most of them in the XI Brigade. One source claims exactly 3,354 Italians of whom 1,819 were Communists—Marcello and Mauricio Ferrara, *Palmiro Togliatti* (Paris, 1955), pp. 268-69. These figures appear reasonable, yet their very precision also makes them suspect. Significantly, neither Longo, Pacciardi, Penchienati, nor Nenni offers any such estimates. Yugoslavs numbered 1,500, of whom almost half reportedly were killed (Vladimir Dedijer, *Tito Speaks*—London, 1953—pp. 107-8), and the number of Hungarians, Bulgarians, Czechs, and Rumanians combined probably approached this figure. There were about 1,000 Canadians in the summer of 1937, and some 3,000 Americans. Rust (p. 210) places the British volunteers at 2,000, of whom 500 were killed and 1,203 wounded, but another Englishman, Neal Wood, estimates British volunteers at 2,762, with 532 killed and 1,762 wounded—*Communism and the British Intellectuals* (London, 1959), p. 56.

These groups total about 34,000, but the precise number of International volunteers may never be known; few records were kept at the beginning, while much of the information compiled thereafter apparently is now in Poland. We have very little data pertaining to the volunteers from the rest of the fifty-three nations allegedly represented in Spain. However, a roster of the Tschapaiew in June 1937 reveals, in addition to virtually all of the aforementioned nationalities, a group of 20 Palestinians, 5 Luxemburgers, a Greek and a Brazilian. References to other nationalities also crop up in the literature, e.g., Cypriots (two Greeks), Cubans, Mexicans, Filipinos, and Chinese. See, for example, "Contribution of Cyprus to the Cause of Spanish Democracy," *The Volunteer for Liberty*, January 13, 1938, p. 10; and "Cuban Volunteers in Spain," *The Volunteer for Liberty*, February 28, 1938, p. 9.

14. "Nuestro voluntarios internacionales: Por qué han venido y por qué se fueron," *Nuestro ejército,* December, 1938, pp. 38-44. See also Wintringham, pp. 327-28; and Rust, pp. 7-8. Official figures made available to Louis Fischer (*Why Spain Fights On*—London, 1938—p. 27) late in 1937 showed that

25,000 volunteers had entered Spain as of October 1, 1937; at least 4,000 were known dead, 14,000-16,000 wounded, and 4,500 repatriated.

15. Wintringham, p. 328. See also Herbert Matthews, *Two Wars and More to Come,* p. 209.

16. Longo (pp. 372-73) places the number of non-Spanish volunteers participating in the Brunete offensive at between 6,000-7,000, and this included every International Brigade except the XIV. Rolfe (p. 8) claims that at no time were there more than 18,000 volunteers in all of Spain, and even at this peak figure, one third were in training and an additional 1,000 in medical and auxiliary services. Never, he contends, were there as many as 7,500 Internationals in battle at any one time. Fischer says that on no single day did the Internationals exceed 15,000 and that there were never more than 9,000 at the front at the same time (*Why Spain Fights On,* p. 27).

17. Longo (p. 216) tells of a meeting of battalion and brigade political commissars during the battle along the Jarama at which the "great discrepancy" between the Internationals and the Spanish soldiers in the matter of arms, equipment, and organization was discussed. The upshot was that the international units were ordered to give up whatever they could to Spanish units. Longo admits the Internationals were not "enthusiastic" about parting with any of their equipment, hardly surprising since even such basic items as cartridges were still in short supply.

18. Stephen Spender, *World Within World* (New York, 1951), p. 193; Romilly, p. 70. But, as Regler (p. 284) points out, many volunteers were anti-fascist emigres who for three years suffered humiliation at the hands of the Paris, Prague, and Swiss police. Some had been required to report daily to apply for another day's asylum.

19. Malraux, *Man's Hope* (New York, 1941), p. 276; Sommerfield, p. 29; Voros, pp. 330-31.

20. Wintringham, p. 114; Longo, *Brigate,* pp. 45, 92, 210-11, 256.

21. F. Dahlem, "The Military-Political Work of the Eleventh International Brigade," *Communist International,* vol. 15, no. 15 (May 1938), p. 450. Longo made a similar comment re-

garding the reception afforded the XIII Brigade when it moved to the Málaga front from Teruel.

22. *Owl of Minerva*, p. 289.
23. Comité pro-niños españoles de las brigadas internacionales, *Los niños españoles y las brigadas internacionales* (Barcelona, 1938). See also "A True Picture of the Volunteers for Liberty," *The Volunteer for Liberty*, November 1, 1937, p. 16; and "Hogar de Niños—Soldiers of the XI Brigade Maintain a Home for Children Who Are Victims of War," *The Volunteer for Liberty*, December 27, 1937, pp. 8-9.
24. Gates, *The Story of an American Communist*, pp. 46-47. See also "American Hospitals Throw a Children's Party," *The Volunteer for Liberty*, September 27, 1937, pp. 4-5.
25. André Marty, "L'Espagne, bastion avancé de la liberté et de la paix," *La brochure populaire No. 3* (Paris, 1937).
26. Rust, p. 6; Douglas Hyde, *I Believed* (New York, 1946), p. 62; Matthews, *Two Wars and More to Come*, p. 207. Rust lists the political affiliation of 460 of the British volunteers killed in Spain (pp. 189-99). Of these, 205 were Communists and 72 Labourites. The political affiliation of the remaining 183 was not indicated, very likely not known.
27. Through its publication, *Socialist Call*, the Socialist Party in 1937 attempted to recruit a Eugene Debs Brigade, but with very little success. Only a few volunteers went to Spain under the direct sponsorship of the Socialist Party. For an account of this and other matters, including the policy of the State Department and the role of the F.B.I., see F. J. Taylor, *The United States and the Spanish Civil War* (New York, 1956).
28. Gates, memorandum, May 1966.
29. General Walter Krivitsky, "Stalin's Hand in Spain," *The Saturday Evening Post*, April 15, 1939, pp. 115-17; Gates, memorandum; Romilly, p. 67; Wintringham, p. 114; Fischer, *Men and Politics*, p. 386. And as Gates points out, the N.K.G.B. seldom had to check recruits, since the volunteers were investigated by the Communist apparatus in their home countries before they ever arrived in Spain.
30. Jesus Hernández Tomás, *Yo fui ministro de Stalin* (Mexico City, 1953), pp. 136-37; André Marty, "The International

Brigade—Twelve Magnificent Months," *International Press Correspondence,* October 20, 1937, pp. 1043-44; "Los voluntarios de la libertad," *Nuestro ejército,* July 1938, p. 26; Fischer, *Men and Politics,* p. 405.

31. José Díaz, "Organizing the Victory of the Spanish People," *The Communist International,* vol. 14, no. 3 (March 1937), pp. 318-31; *La politica militar del P.O.U.M.* (Barcelona, 1937), pp. 8, 23.

32. Comité pro niños españoles.

33. Voros, pp. 409-10; Communist Party of the Soviet Union, *The Land of Socialism Today and Tomorrow* (Moscow, 1939), p. 92.

CHAPTER 6

1. Gates, *Story of an American Communist,* p. 47; memorandum to author.

2. *Bulletin of the Political Commissars of the International Brigades,* No. 3 (September 1937), p. 27.

3. *Ibid.,* pp. 29-30.

4. Enrique Castro Delgado, "Los relaciones del comisario con el mando," *Nuestro ejército,* October 1938, p. 6.

5. B. F. Osorio Tafall, "Los comisarios en el ejército de la independencia de España," *Nuestro ejército,* July 1938, p. 6; A. F. Vittori, "The War Against Illiteracy," *Bulletin of the Political Commissars of the International Brigades,* September 1937, p. 24.

6. Longo, pp. 243-44, 250.

7. "Bureaucracy and the Commissar," *The Bulletin of the Political Commissars of the International Brigades,* September 1937, pp. 16-17.

8. Enrique Castro Delgado, "Las tareas de los comisarios en la fase actual de la guerra," *Nuestro ejército,* June 1938, p. 21; "Plan of Short Courses for Political Delegates," *Bulletin of the Political Commissars of the International Brigades,* October-November, 1937, pp. 12, 30-31.

9. Bolloten, pp. 291, 309, 312; F. Dahlem, "The Military-Political

Work of the Eleventh International Brigade," *The Communist International,* May 1938, p. 450.

10. Fischer, *Men and Politics,* p. 455.

11. The complete text of the decree was published in *The Volunteer for Liberty* on November 1, 1937, "Our International Brigades," pp. 12-15. See also Rolfe, pp. 145-48.

12. Gates, memorandum.

13. Gates, memorandum; Alvarez del Vayo, *Freedom's Battle,* pp. 127-28.

14. Gates, memorandum. The confusion of responsibility inherent in the commissar system is reflected in Mr. Gates' memorandum written almost thirty years later: He used the term "units under my command."

15. "Marcel," "The Fifth Column," *Bulletin of the Political Commissars of the International Brigades,* September 1937, p. 13. See also M. Arpi-Loza, "The Fight Against Provocation and Espionage in the Peoples' Army," *ibid.,* October-November, 1937, p. 25.

16. Penchienati, pp. 39-43. Penchienati, a "non-party" man, commanded a battalion of the XII Brigade while Pacciardi was brigade commander and subsequently succeeded to the brigade command. His book gives one of the best accounts of the machinations of the Communists in the International Brigades.

17. Organizzazione Vigilanza Reati Antifascista, or Organization for Vigilance against Anti-fascist Crimes—the Fascist secret police.

18. The C.N.T., or Confederación Nacional de Trabajo, was an even larger organization than the Socialist Unión General de Trabajadores (U.G.T.). Probably the best history of the Anarchist movement in Spain is that of Gerald Brenan, *The Spanish Labyrinth* (London, 1950).

19. Definitive statements of the P.O.U.M. position are those of Felix Morrow, *Revolution and Counter-Revolution in Spain* (New York, 1938), and Julián Gorkín, *Canibales políticos* (Mexico, 1941). These works cover the whole sequence of events culminating in the suppression of the P.O.U.M. and the aftermath. See also Lambda, *The Truth About the*

Barcelona Events (New York, 1937), and Bertram D. Wolfe, *Civil War in Spain* (New York, 1937). A good statement of the Anarchist position is that of Augustin Souchy, *The Tragic Week in May* (Barcelona, 1937). A "documented" record of "treachery" by the P.O.U.M. is that of George Soria, *Trotskism in the Service of Franco* (New York, 1937?). See also Longo, pp. 330-35.

20. John McGovern, *Terror in Spain* (London, 1938), p. 5. Peter Elstob, *Spanish Prisoner* (New York, 1939); Johan Brouwer, pp. 140-72.

21. Hernández, p. 126; Alexander Orlov, *The Secret History of Stalin's Crimes* (New York, 1953), p. xii. Orlov has plenty to say about intrigue in the Soviet Union, but very little about his own activities in Spain during this period. Hugh Thomas is somewhat dubious about his account, but this reticence argues for its authenticity.

22. Penchienati, pp. 60-63; Pacciardi, pp. 215-17, and letter to the author, April 17, 1952.

23. Gates, *Story of an American Communist,* p. 53, and memorandum.

24. André Marty, "The International Fighters for Freedom Show the Path to Victory Lies in Anti-Fascist Unity," *The Volunteer for Liberty,* November 1, 1937, p. 10; Gates, memorandum. See also "More POUMists Nabbed as Spies," *The Volunteer for Liberty,* August 16, 1937, p. 3, and "Trotskyite Traitors," *ibid.,* September 13, 1937, pp. 9-10. Szinda (p. 106) later condemned the Socialists as well as the "Trotskyites": "The Social Democratic leaders saw their main task in restraining the growing influence of the Communist Party," and made of their own groups "a police force"! But this was twenty-two years after Moscow discarded the popular front.

25. Regler, *Owl of Minerva,* pp. 277-78, 353; see also *The Great Crusade,* pp. 300-302.

26. Penchienati, pp. 26-27, 41-42.

27. Gates, memorandum; Valentín González (El Campesino), *Life and Death in Soviet Russia* (New York, 1952), pp. 22-23. See also Gillain, p. 110; Fischer, *Men and Politics;* Colonel

185

Jesús Pérez Salas, *Guerra en España* (Mexico, D.F., 1947); and Enrique Castro Delgado, *J'ai perdu la foi a Moscou* (Paris, 1950).

CHAPTER 7

1. This was subsequently admitted by Hernández, pp. 78-85. See also Casado, pp. 68-73.
2. See, for example, Longo, *Brigate,* pp. 337-39, and *Épopée,* pp. 120-21.
3. Longo, *Brigate,* p. 339. This Loyalist operation has received more attention from a writer of fiction than from any military historian. Yet few readers of *For Whom the Bell Tolls* realize that Hemingway's classic is set against the background of an actual military operation. The central character, Robert Jordan, a young American idealist (not a Communist), is charged with the task of blowing up the bridge just as the Loyalist offensive is launched. "Robert Jordan," like Robert Merriman, had been an instructor at a western college. Many of the other personages in the story were not fictional—André Marty and General Rojo, for example—while Hemingway knew personally several others, e.g. General "Golz," in reality General "Walter," (Karol Swierczewski). Hemingway wrote the foreword to Regler's *The Great Crusade,* and Regler claims that he provided some of the material used in Hemingway's novel. "I gave him secret material relating to the Party, which he respected because it was fighting more actively than any other body, although he despised its Martys" (*Owl of Minerva,* p. 293).
4. Nenni claims that everything possible was done to alleviate the fears of the population, but Longo (pp. 345-46) indicates that they were not entirely without foundation. While the Internationals were en route to the front, recruits from the Communist Komsomol Battalion joined them, thinking that they were going to fight the Anarchists. Penchienati (p. 106) states that late in October during the Belchite campaign a Catalonian

battalion exchanged shots with some Internationals and was disarmed by two battalions of the XIII Brigade.

5. See "General Lukacs is Dead, He Died a Leader and a Hero of the International Brigades," *The Volunteer for Liberty,* June 22, 1937, p. 2. Lukacz apparently was very popular with non-Communists, even though he was himself a member of the Party. It will be recalled that he sanctioned Pacciardi's arrest of officers who attempted to intervene against the Anarchists during the Barcelona "May Days." Pacciardi refers to him as "my friend."

6. Penchienati, pp. 69-70. Longo identifies General "Belov" as one "F. Kosovski," alias "Petrov." Kleber actually may not have put in an appearance until the last day or so of the operation.

7. Nenni (pp. 178-79), who was wounded in the hand, states that everyone was confused and that rebel aircraft and artillery zeroed in on the "Gramsci" battery with devastating results. This had something to do with the lack of effective support from the Loyalists own artillery.

8. Furious over the lack of artillery and aerial support, Pacciardi protested vigorously to the Political Commissariat at Albacete, which responded by placing two Moscow-trained Communists, Vittorio Mallozi and a Captain Raimondi, in command of two of his battalions. Longo (pp. 344-46) blames inadequate artillery support, poor intelligence (Republican commanders had inadequate knowledge of the terrain), and inadequate reserves.

9. Felix Morrow (p. 165) asserts that three days after the fall of Bilbao, the P.O.U.M. 29th Division (not yet dissolved) was ordered into an attack near Huesca with the promise of flank support from a "Stalinist" International Brigade, but that this support, as well as promised air and artillery support, did not materialize. Nonetheless, the P.O.U.M. troops went into the attack, fully aware that they were being deliberately exposed, in order to avoid being charged with treason.

10. Rojo, *España heroica,* pp. 97-104.

11. Quoted by Marcel Acier, *From Spanish Trenches* (New York, 1937), pp. 138, 165.

12. Rojo, *España heroica,* p. 104; Longo, pp. 373-75; *Épopée,* pp. 128-30; Szinda, p. 56; *Der österreichische Freiwillige,* pp. 35-37. Pacciardi (pp. 231-32), nursing a badly wrenched ankle from the mishap at Huesca, directed his brigade from a stretcher. He claims that the order sending his men into battle so soon after Huesca was "absurd." The brigade had received about 800 Spanish replacements—without arms or uniforms—and Longo (p. 387) seems to blame Pacciardi for sending them into "an inferno" without any military or "political" training.

13. Kantorowicz, *Tschapaiew,* pp. 175-76; Rust, pp. 74-75; Rolfe, p. 91. The new commander of the Lincolns was a Texas Negro and Communist, Oliver Law. According to Herbert Matthews, he was a "good businessman to boot, having owned a restaurant and other property which he gave up to come to Spain" (*Two Wars and More to Come,* p. 217).

14. Lojendio, p. 331. Longo states that twenty-three "International" artillery batteries participated in the Brunete campaign.

15. Penchienati, p. 78.

16. This is Rolfe's version; Rust (p. 76) claims that the original plan called for the entire XV Brigade to "march into the town after it had been captured by another Brigade, but the town had not yet fallen." The "other brigade" appears to have been the XIII, which ran into considerable difficulty. The American Communist Steve Nelson adds that "Back in brigade headquarters there was bitterness and cursing. It had not been intended for the Fifteenth to attack Cañada; that was for another unit." (Steve Nelson, *The Volunteers*—New York, 1953—p. 148.)

17. Rolfe, p. 92; Rust, p. 77. Rust says that the British unit's canteens had been sent to be filled just before the offensive began, and the men soon found themselves in a desperate state.

18. Rojo, *España heroica,* pp. 105, 110. See also F. Dahlem, "The Military-Political Work of the Eleventh International Brigade," *The Communist International,* May 1938, p. 452. Franquist sources claim that the XIII refused to obey orders and was later dissolved. The basis for their contention appears to be the account of Nick Gillain (pp. 131-55), but it is not clear that

Gillain was actually present. Casado (p. 75) says the brigade had asked to be relieved due to its "extraordinary state of exhaustion," but the request was refused. Longo (pp. 384-87) states that the XIII Brigade came up from the Estremadura front believing that it was going into rest, and instead was thrown into the "furnace." Although it suffered heavier losses than any of the other international units at Brunete, Longo claims that the brigade "didn't lose a meter of ground." When queried by the author, some Spaniards who had participated in the Brunete offensive confirmed Casado's contention and left no doubt as to the chaos created by the air attacks. Moe Fishman, Secretary of the Veterans of the Abraham Lincoln Brigade, advised the writer that to the best of his knowledge and of some others who had participated in the Brunete campaign there was no mutiny in any unit (letter to the writer, April 17, 1952). Alvah Bessie advised the writer that isolated units, from squad to company size, might have broken and retreated, but he never heard of a major "mutiny" or rout of any kind (letter to the writer, April 7, 1952). Without naming any specific unit, the *Volunteer for Liberty* mentioned a unit at Brunete which "yielded to panic" although "scarcely under fire" ("After the Sierra—What?," August 9, 1937, p. 1).

19. Rolfe, pp. 97-98, 105-6; Rust, p. 85; Szinda, p. 56; Steve Nelson (p. 170), who assumed command of the Lincolns after the death of Oliver Law, makes it clear that the order to return to the front elicited anything but enthusiasm; as one commissar allegedly put it: "Christ, man, you can't get blood out of a stone."

20. Casado, p. 73; Rojo, *España heroica,* p. 110.

21. Penchienati, p. 91.

22. Penchienati, pp. 90-104; Nenni, p. 181. "Untroubled by nerves or fear," a "leader of exceptional intelligence," "self assured, dominating, never dismayed by human frailty"—thus Regler describes Pacciardi (*Owl of Minerva,* p. 290).

23. Rojo, *España heroica,* p. 120. Although called the "Belchite offensive," the appellation may have been applied because of the failure to take the principal objective, Saragossa. See Penchienati, p. 98, and Pérez Salas, p. 153.

24. Rolfe, pp. 116-20; Szinda, p. 61; Wullschleger, pp. 209-12. See also "Fifth Army Corps Documents Aragon Advance," *The Volunteer for Liberty,* September 13, 1937, p. 3.

25. Ernest Hemingway, *The Spanish War* (London, 1938), p. 35; Rojo, *España heroica,* p. 127. A very interesting account of the defense of the town is that of a Nationalist officer who was there: Capitan de Diego, *Belchite* (Barcelona, 1939).

26. At one point Kleber's troops allegedly got to within two and a half miles of Saragossa (*Épopée,* p. 136), while Lister's troops penetrated to within one mile of the provincial capital (Rolfe, p. 122).

27. "The History of the MacKenzie-Papineau Battalion," *The Volunteer for Liberty,* November 7, 1938, pp. 4-5. Also Rolfe, pp. 133-34.

28. Hemingway, *Spanish War,* p. 36; *Épopée,* p. 138. See also "Ernest Hemingway Tells of American Volunteers in Aragon," *The New York Times,* September 14, 1937, p. 10; and Herbert Matthews, "Belchite Operation Reviewed," *The New York Times,* September 19, 1937, p. 33.

29. Gates, *American Communist,* p. 51; Penchienati, p. 114.

30. Rojo, *España heroica,* pp. 120, 122, 127; Buckley, p. 384; Zugazagoitia, p. 318; Rust, p. 96.

CHAPTER 8

1. The intelligence reports were correct. See Lojendio, p. 367.

2. *Épopée,* p. 140; Lojendio, pp. 361-95; Aznar, pp. 546-85.

3. Szinda (p. 65) emphasizes the misery of the troops who were not equipped with winter clothing. But Rolfe (p. 172) indicates that the Americans had an opportunity to augment their supplies of clothing while quartered in Teruel: "the well stocked stores supplied fantastic clothes to take the place of their ragged uniforms. It was not unusual to see hundreds of men walking about in patent leather shoes, striped vests, and an odd assortment of trousers, coats and ties."

4. Rolfe, pp. 164, 169, 170.

5. González, pp. 26, 28-29.

6. Rojo, *España heroica,* pp. 149-52.

7. Rolfe, pp. 184-87; Lojendio, p. 451; Aznar, p. 630; Alvah Bessie, *Men in Battle* (New York, 1939), p. 117 (probably the best personal narrative of one who fought in Spain); Voros, pp. 391-92.

8. There is very little information about the activities of the XII Brigade during this period. Penchienati (p. 108) says that after the Aragon campaign in the fall of 1937, the brigade was sent to Albacete and in March shifted to Estremadura where it participated in an abortive offensive.

9. Rolfe, pp. 197-98; Lojendio, p. 472; Aznar, p. 637; *Épopée,* pp. 146-50. Szinda (p. 68) states that in its retreat to Caspe the XI Brigade lost over a thousand men. See also the account of Konrad Schmidt, who was in the Hans Beimler Battalion and was taken prisoner, in Wullschleger, pp. 286-96.

10. Rolfe, pp. 208-25; Rust, pp. 140-61; Wintringham, p. 307.

11. Rojo, *España heroica,* pp. 134-38.

12. Quoted by Zugazagoitia, p. 379. For Prieto's own account, see *Cómo y por qué salí del ministerio de defensa nacional* (Mexico City, 1940).

13. Henríquez Caubín, *La batalla del Ebro,* pp. 33-34. This account, by the chief of staff of the 35th Division, is one of the best Republican works available on a single campaign.

14. Bessie, pp. 148-49, 334.

15. The International Brigade authorities first turned down Lardner's request to enlist, but finally decided to let him join, partly because he was so insistent, and partly because of his propaganda value. To avoid any risk to his life, however, he was sent to a camp at Badalona in Catalonia, a camp for the *inútiles de guerra*—the unfit. Lardner left the camp, and through the intercession of John Gates succeeded in joining the Lincoln Battalion, which was then being reorganized near Mora la Nueva north of the Ebro. See Vincent Sheean, *Not Peace but a Sword* (New York, 1939), pp. 248-53.

16. Rolfe, pp. 247-48; Rojo, *España heroica,* p. 172.

17. Alvarez del Vayo, *Freedom's Battle,* p. 134; Gates, memorandum.

191

18. Bessie, p. 172; Gates, memorandum. Rolfe (pp. 245-46) also mentions "news heavily larded with exaggerated rumors" of an impending repatriation of the volunteers.

   During the retreat in Aragon, the Cheka seems to have exacted a toll of its own among the volunteers, particularly among the Poles, Slavs, Germans, and Hungarians (Voros, pp. 410-13). And Gates, as noted previously, states that the one execution of an American in the units *under his command* occurred after the retreat in the spring of 1938. In the next three months, he says, he frequently had to sentence men to a few days in the guardhouse (Gates, memorandum). Penchienati (pp. 108-13) claims that after the headquarters of the Internationals was moved from Albacete to Barcelona, special prisons were set up by the Cheka at Cambrils, Horta, and Castelldefels. He personally witnessed a scene in which a hundred or so worn-out survivors of the Aragon debacle were harangued by Marty at Cambrils, and in the course of which Marty beat several of them on the head with his pistol. He also asserts that at this time executions among Lister's and Campesino's troops were "ferocious" and that Lister even ordered the execution of Internationals.

   Bessie (pp. 148-49) maintains that few of the Internationals deserted, but at least two of those who did managed to create quite a stir. In testimony before a Congressional committee in August 1938, two former members of the Lincoln Battalion, Abraham Sobel and A. L. Halpern, declared that ninety per cent of the Americans in Spain wanted to come home but were prevented from doing so by the Communists (*New York Times,* August 19, 21, 1938). And an American correspondent, Edward Knoblaugh, also encountered two deserters, one Canadian, the other Irish, who claimed that "hundreds" of Internationals wanted to leave Spain but did not have passports (*Correspondent in Spain*—London, 1937—pp. 227-28). Even though such deserters' testimony should be discounted, most of the Internationals had undoubtedly lost their earlier enthusiasm by the summer of 1938.

19. Rojo, *España heroica,* p. 169; Pérez Salas, pp. 209-12; Alvarez del Vayo, *Freedom's Battle,* p. 138.

20. The XV Brigade was under the command of a Spaniard, José Maria Valledor, who had replaced Vladimir Čopic. Just what became of Čopic is not known.

21. *Épopée,* pp. 154-55; Henríquez Caubín, pp. 33-34; Szinda, pp. 76-78; Wullschleger, p. 221; Fischer, *Men and Politics,* p. 543; "With the Lincoln-Washington," *The Volunteer for Liberty,* August 26, 1938, pp. 4-5.

22. League of Nations, *Official Journal: Special Supplement No. 183* (Geneva, 1938), p. 90; *Special Supplement No. 189,* p. 65; League of Nations, *Official Journal,* "Minutes of the the Hundred-and-Fourth Session of the Council" (Geneva, 1939), p. 124. The withdrawal of the Internationals of course had but little effect on the fighting capacity of the Republican Army. About 700,000 men were mobilized; the problem was arms and equipment.

23. Ernest Hemingway, *Somebody Had to Do Something* (Los Angeles, 1939); Sheean, pp. 265-66; Rolfe, pp. 289-91.

24. Voros, p. 441. Prior to the farewell parade, Voros prevailed upon some members of the Anarchist "Mujeres Libres" (Free Women) to participate in a fiesta put on by the XV Brigade. The women were at first quite cool to the idea as they considered the Internationals mostly Communists. Much to the disappointment of the volunteers, the Spanish women who finally decided to attend turned out to be anything but the type of "free women" they had hoped for.

25. In an editorial for *The Volunteer,* Voros congratulated the Internationals on their opportunity to go to the Soviet Union. He received a stinging reprimand from Marty. The editorial was not printed, and the U.S.S.R. did not open its gates to the rank and file of the volunteers. (Voros, p. 443.)

26. The commission didn't find all the prisoners. Penchienati (pp. 124-43) claims that when he got word to Prime Minister Negrín about the activities of the Cheka at Horta and Castelldefels—where several hundred prisoners were detained and scores executed—Negrín dispatched the Spanish S.I.M. to arrest those responsible. In December, Penchienati himself participated in a raid on the prison at Horta in which a number of prisoners were liberated.

193

27. League of Nations, *Official Journal,* 1939, "Minutes of the Hundred-and-Fourth Session of the Council," pp. 126-31.

28. Henry Buckley (p. 416) was at the border on January 30 when French *Gardes Mobiles* herded wounded Loyalist soldiers back across the border. When the border was finally opened on February 3, the Spanish refugees and non-French Internationals were crowded into concentration camps which had no buildings, firewood, or adequate sanitary facilities. Herbert Matthews visited one camp in which 25,000 refugees were confined without a single latrine (*The Education of a Correspondent,* p. 186; see also *Épopée,* pp. 176-79).

29. Matthews, *Education of a Correspondent,* pp. 185-86. This group of Internationals consisted of some 150 Americans, Canadians, and Englishmen, 300 Italians, and 250 Czechs and other Slavs. On the following day, 1,200 Internationals crossed the border, mostly Poles, Germans, and Austrians of the XI and XIII Brigades. Regler, too, mentions the volunteers who crossed into France singing, but claims that Marty, with a group of about ten colleagues, was about to liquidate a larger group with whom they had been marching. Klaus Becher, a former artillery officer at Albacete under Marty, was with the larger group, and told Regler that he felt Marty was going to have his contingent machine-gunned because they "knew too much." Becher consequently told his group to keep their arms at the ready, and it was in this state, with some seventy-five drawn up into a phalanx, that they were spotted by Regler.

CHAPTER 9

1. Subversive Activities Control Board, Docket No. 108-53; Herbert Brownell Jr., Attorney General of the United States, Petitioner v. Veterans of the Abraham Lincoln Brigade, Respondent. *Report and Order of the Board,* Decided December 21, 1955. In its report, the board also noted the unsuccessful efforts of some of the volunteers to form a rival Veterans of the Abraham Lincoln Brigade—Anti-Totalitarian.

2. Subversive Activities Control Board, p. 59.

3. Introduction to bound volume of *The Volunteer for Liberty* (New York, 1948), pp. ii-iii.
4. Subversive Activities Control Board, p. 89.
5. Salvador de Madariaga, *Spain,* p. 384.

Bibliography

Acier, Marcel. *From Spanish Trenches.* New York: Modern Age Books, 1937.

Algarra Rafegas, Comandante Antonio. *El asedio de Huesca.* Saragossa: Editoriales "El Noticiero," 1941.

Alonso, Bruno. *La flota republicana y la guerra civil de España.* Mexico City: Imprenta Graficos, 1944.

Alvarez del Vayo. *Freedom's Battle.* New York: Alfred Knopf, 1940.

————. *The Last Optimist.* New York: The Viking Press, 1950.

Among Friends (New York: Friends of the Abraham Lincoln Brigade), various issues 1937-38.

Anton, Francisco. *Madrid, orgullo de la España anti-fascista.* [Madrid?] 1937.

Araquistáin Quevedo, Luis. *El comunismo y la guerra de España.* Carmaux (France), 1939.

Arpi Loza, M. "The Fight Against Provocation and Espionage in the Peoples' Army," *Bulletin of the Political Commissars of the International Brigades.* No. 3, September, 1937.

Arrarás, Joaquín (ed.). *Historia de la cruzada Española* (35 volumes). Madrid: 1939-43.

Arrese, Domingo de. *La España de Franco.* Madrid: Publicaciones Españolas, 1947.

Asensio Torrado, General José. *El General Asensio: Su lealtad a la república.* Barcelona, 1938.

Aznar, Manuel. *Historia militar de la guerra de España (1936-1939).* Madrid: Ediciones Idea, 1940.

Balk, Theodore (ed.). *La Quatorzième.* Madrid: Editions du Commissariat des Brigadas Internacionales, 1937.

Barea, Arturo. *The Clash*. London: Faber and Faber, 1946.

———. *Valor y miedo*. Barcelona, 1938.

La Batalla (Newspaper, Barcelona).

[Anon.] *Ben Leider, American Hero: He Died Fighting for Democracy*. New York (1937?).

Beriford-Jones. *Student Under Arms: Education in Republican Spain*. New York, 1938.

Bertrán Güell, Felipe. *Preparación y desarrollo del alzamiento nacional*. Valladolid: Libreria Santaren, 1939.

Bessie, Alvah. Letter to the author.

———. *Men in Battle*. New York: Scribner's Sons, 1939.

Beumelberg Werner. *Kampf um Spanien*. Berlin: G. Stalling 1940.

Blum, Ignacy. *Z Dziejow Aparatu politycznego Wojska polskiego: Szkicefi dokumenty*. Warsaw: Wydawn Ministerstwa Obrony Narodowej, 1957.

Boletín de Informacion (Barcelona, C.N.T.-A.I.T.-F.A.I.), various issues, 1937.

Boletín de informacion de las brigadas internacionales del ejército popular español (mimeograph), various issues.

Bolloten, Burnett. *The Grand Camouflage: The Communist Conspiracy in the Spanish Civil War*. New York: Frederick Praeger, 1961.

Borkenau, Franz. *The Spanish Cockpit*. London: Faber and Faber, 1937.

Bowers, Claude G. *My Mission to Spain: Watching the Rehearsal for World War II*. New York: Simon and Schuster, 1954.

Brenan, Gerald, *The Spanish Labyrinth: An Account of the Social and Political Background of the Civil War*. 2nd Edition. London: Cambridge University Press, 1950.

Las brigadas internacionales según testimonio de sus artífices. Barcelona: Comité de informacion y actuación social [1939?].

Brome, Vincent. *The International Brigades*. New York: Morrow, 1966.

Bron, Michal. *Polacy w Wojnie hiszpanskiej 1936-1939*. Warsaw: Wydawn Ministerstwa Obrony narodowij, 1963.

———. *Wojna hiszpanska 1936-1939*. Warsaw: Panstwowe Zaklady Wud wn Szkolmysh, 1961.

Brongersma, E. *Voorproef in Spanje, 1919-1939*. Utrecht and Brussel: Uitgeverij Het Spectrum, 1946.

Broué, Pierre, and Témime, Emile. *La révolution et la guerre D'Espagne*. Paris: Editions de Minuit, 1961.

Brouwer, Johan. *In den Schaduw van den Dood*. Zutphen: W. J. Thieme [1946?].

Buckley, Henry W. *Life and Death of the Spanish Republic*. London: H. Hamilton, 1940.

Bulletin of the Political Commissars of the International Brigades. Various issues, 1937.

"Bureaucracy and the Commissar," *Bulletin of the Political Commissars of the International Brigades*, No. 3, September, 1937.

Cacho Zabalza, Antonio. *La unión militar española*. Alicante: Egasa, 1940.

Cantalupo, Roberto. *Fu la Spagna*. Milan: A Mondadori, 1948.

Cardozo, Harold G. *The March of a Nation*. London: Eyre and Spottiswoode, 1937.

Casado, Segismundo. *The Last Days of Madrid: The End of the Second Spanish Republic*. Translated by Rupert Croft-Cooke. London: P. Davies, 1939.

Castro Delgado, Enrique. *J'ai perdu la foi a Moscou*. Paris: Librarie Gallimard, 1950.

———. "Las Relaciones del Comisario con el Mando Militar," *Nuestro ejército*, October 1938.

Cattell, David T. *Communism and the Spanish Civil War*. Berkeley and Los Angeles: University of California Press, 1956.

Clavego, P. E. *El trabajo de los comisarios politicos*. Barcelona: Ediciones Europa-America [1937?].

Colodny, Robert Garland. *The Struggle For Madrid: The Central Epic of the Spanish Conflict (1936-1937)*. New York: Paine-Whitman, 1958.

Comité pro-niños españoles de las brigadas internacionales. *Los niños españoles y las brigadas internacionales*. Barcelona: Tipografica Catalana E.C., 1938.

Committee of Inquiry Into Breaches of International Law Relating to Intervention in Spain. *Report and Findings*. London: W. H. Taylor and Sons, 1936.

The Communist International (New York), various issues, 1936-39).

The Communist International. "Decision of the Presidium of the Executive Committee of the Communist International on the Work of the Communist Party of Spain," *The Communist International,* vol. 14, no. 2, February 1937.

————. *Unity for Spain: Correspondence Between the Communist International and the Labor and Socialist International, June–July 1937.* New York: Workers Library Publisher, 1937.

Communist Party of the Soviet Union. *The Land of Socialism Today and Tomorrow: Reports and Speeches at the Eighteenth Congress of the Communist Party of the Soviet Union, March 10-21, 1939.* Moscow: Foreign Language Publishing House, 1939.

Confederacion nacional de trabajo—Federacion anarquista ibérica. *Estampas de la revolucion española, 19 julio de 1936.* Barcelona: Talleres Graficas, Colectivizada [1937?].

Cowles, Virginia, *Looking for Trouble.* New York and London: Harper and Brothers, 1941.

Cox, Geoffrey. *Defence of Madrid.* London: Gollancz (Left Book Club edition), 1937.

Dahlem, F. "The Military-Political Work of the Eleventh International Brigade," *The Communist International,* vol. 15, no. 15, May 1938.

Dallet, Joe. *Joe Dallet: Letters From Spain: From an American Volunteer to His Wife.* Introduction by Wm. Z. Foster and Earl Browder. New York: Workers Library Publisher, 1938.

Dean, Vera Micheles. "European Diplomacy in the Spanish Civil Strife," *Geneva Special Studies,* VII (1936), no. 8.

Dedijer, Vladimir. *Tito Speaks.* London: Weidenfeld, 1953.

Defensa nacional: Revista española de tecnica militar (Madrid), infrequently issued, 1937.

De la Mora, Constancia. *In Place of Splendor.* New York: Harcourt, Brace and Company, 1939.

Delaprée. Luis. *The Martyrdom of Madrid.* Madrid, 1937.

Del Barrio, José. *Open-Brief aan het politiek Bureau van het centraal Comite der Spaanse communistische Partij.* [Amsterdam?] mimeographed, 1950.

Delegacion nacional de prensa y propaganda de falange española tradicionalista y de las J.O.N.S. *Intervención del marxismo internacional en la guerra de España: testimonio de combatientes rojos.* Bibao: Editoria Nacional, 1939.

Deschamps, Bernard. *La vérité sur Guadalajara.* Paris: Donoel, 1938.

De Wet, Oloff. *The Patrol Is Ended.* New York: Doubleday, Doran and Co., 1938.

Díaz, José. "Organizing the Victory of the Spanish People," *The Communist International,* vol. 14, No. 3, March 1937.

————. *Tres años de lucha.* Bar-le-Duc (France), 1939.

De Diego, Capitan. *Belchite.* Barcelona: Editoria Nacional, 1939.

Dietrich, Erich. *Kriegsschule Toledo.* Leipzig: Koehler & Amelang, 1937.

Dimitrov, Georgi. *Two Years of Heroic Struggle of the Spanish People.* New York: Workers Library Publisher, 1938.

Dom Wojska polskiego. *General Karol Swierczewski.* Warsaw: [Wojskowy Instytut Naukowo Wydwaniczy ?], 1950.

El comisario: Revista semanal político-militar del comisariato general de guerra (Valencia), various issues, 1937.

El ejército popular (Barcelona), various issues, 1937.

Elliot, John. "With the Rebels," *Atlantic Monthly,* November 1936.

Elstob, Peter. *Spanish Prisoner.* New York: Carrick and Evans, 1939.

Épopée d'Espagne: Brigades internationales 1936-1939. 2d edition. Paris: L'Amicale des anciens volontaires Française en Espagne républicane, 1957.

Ercoli, M. (Palmiro Togliatti). *The Spanish Revolution.* New York: Workers Library Publisher, 1936.

Esch, P.A.M. van der. *Prelude to War: The International Repercussions of the Spanish Civil War, 1936-1939.* The Hague: Martinus Nijhoff, 1951.

"Fallen in Battle," *The Communist International,* vol. 14, no. 1, January 1937.

"Far Reaching Effects of the Ebro Offensive," *The Communist International,* vol. 15, no. 9, September 1938.

Felix-Maiz, B. *Alzamiento en España.* 2nd edition. Pamplona, 1952.

Ferrara, Marcello and Mauricio. *Palmiro Togliatti,* Paris: Editions Sociales, 1955.

Fischer, Louis. *Men and Politics.* London: Jonathan Cape, 1941.

————. "Spain's 'Red' Foreign Legion," *The Nation,* January 9, 1937.

————. *The War in Spain.* New York: Spanish Information Bureau, 1937.

————. *Why Spain Fights On.* London: Union of Democratic Control, 1938.

Fishman, Moe. Letter to the author, April 17, 1952.

Foss, William, and Gerahty, Cecil. *The Spanish Arena.* London: John Gifford, Ltd. 1938.

Foxá y Torroba, Augustin. *Madrid: De corte a cheka.* San Sebastian: Libreria Internacional, 1938.

Franco y Bahamonde, Francisco. *Franco ha dicho.* Madrid: Ediciones Voz, 1948.

————. *Speech Delivered by the Head of the State at the Opening of the Third Legislative Session of the Spanish Cortes on May 18, 1949.* Madrid: Spanish Information Office, 1949.

Fraser, Hamish. *De las brigadas internacionales a los sindicatos católicos.* Madrid: Editoria Nacional, 1957.

Friedlander, Robert A. "Great Power Politics and Spain's Civil War: The First Phase," *The Historian,* xxviii, no. 1, November 1965.

————. Letter to the author.

Frondaie, Pierre. *Le volontaire.* Paris: Librarie Plon, 1938.

Fuhr, Lini. "I Was a Nurse in Loyalist Spain," *Among Friends* (New York), Spring, 1938.

Gannes, Harry. *How the Soviet Union Helps Spain.* New York: Workers Library Publisher 1936.

Gannes, Harry, and Repard, Theodore. *Spain in Revolt.* New York: Alfred Knopf, 1937.

Garcia Pradas. *La traición de Stalin: Como termino la guerra de España.* New York: Ediciones de cultura proletaria, 1939.

Gates, John. Memorandum on draft of present volume, May 14, 1966.

———. *The Story of an American Communist*. New York: Thomas Nelson and Sons, 1958.

Georges-Roux. *La guerre civile d'Espagne*. Paris: Librarie Artheme Fayard, 1963.

Gillain, Nick. *Le mercenaire*. Paris: F. Brouty and A. Fayard, 1938.

González, Valentín, and Gorkín, Julián. *El Campesino: Life and Death in Soviet Russia*. Translated by Ilsa Barea. New York: G. P. Putnam's Sons, 1952.

Gorkín, Julián. *Canibales políticos: Hitler y Stalin en España*. Mexico, D. F.: Ediciones Quetzal, 1941.

Great Britain, House of Commons. *Accounts and Papers, State Papers, Spain No. 2 (1936)*, cmd. 5300, vol. xxvii (The Legislative and Other Measures Taken by the Participating Governments to Give Effect to the Agreement Regarding Non-Intervention in Spain, and by the Swiss Government to Prohibit the Export and Carriage of Arms and War Material from Switzerland to Spain). London, 1936.

———. *Accounts and Papers, State Papers, Spain No. 1 (1937)*, cmd. 5399, vol. xxviii (Resolution Adopted by the International Committee for the Application of the Agreement Regarding Non-Intervention in Spain Relating to a Scheme of Observation of the Spanish Frontier by Land and Sea, March 8, 1937). London, 1937.

———. *Accounts and Papers, State Papers (1936-1937)*, cmd. 5570, vol. xxix (Correspondence With the Italian Government Regarding the Withdrawal of Foreign Volunteers From Spain, October 2-9, 1937). London, 1937.

———. *Accounts and Papers, State Papers, Spain No. 1 (1938)*, cmd. 5793, vol. xxx (Text of a Proposed Resolution Reaffirming and Extending the Non-Intervention Agreement, and Providing for the Withdrawal of Foreign Volunteers from Spain, for the Grant, in Certain Circumstances, of Belligerent Rights to the Two Parties in Spain, and for the Observation of the Spanish Frontiers by Land and Sea, July 5, 1938). London, 1938.

———. *Parliamentary Debates*. London, continuing series.

Grondijs, L. H. *Spanje—een Voortzetting van de russische Revolutie?* Leiden: A. W. Sithoffs, Uitgeverij, N. V., 1937.

203

Guzman, Eduardo de. *Madrid, rojo y negro.* Barcelona: Editorial Tierra y Libertad, 1938.

Hart, Merwin. *America, Look at Spain.* New York: D. J. Kenedy and Sons, 1939.

Hemingway, Ernest. *For Whom the Bell Tolls.* New York: Chas. Scribner's Sons, 1940.

Hemingway, Ernest. *The Spanish War.* London: Fact, 1938.

———, and others. *Somebody Had To Do Something: A Memorial to James Phillips Lardner, by Ernest Hemingway, Ring Lardner, Jr., Jay Allen, Jesus Hernandez, El Campesino, Dolores Ibarruri, Vincent Sheean.* Los Angeles: The James Lardner Memorial Fund, 1939.

Henríquez Caubín, Julián. *La batalla del Ebro.* Mexico, D. F.: Unda y Garcia, 1944.

Hericourt, Pierre. *Arms for Red Spain.* London: Burns, Oates and Washburn, 1938.

———. *Pourquoi mentir? L'aide franco-soviétique a l'Espagne rouge.* Paris: Editions Baudinier, 1937.

Hernández Tomás, Jesús. *Yo fui ministro de Stalin.* Mexico City: Editorial America, 1953.

Hood and Frankfeld. *Americans in Spain: New England Fights for Spanish Democracy.* Boston: Communist Party of New England, 1938.

Hudson, R. B. *True Americans: A Tribute to American Maritime Workers Who Fought for World Democracy in the Trenches of Spain.* New York: Workers Library Publisher, 1939.

L'Humanité (newspaper, Paris).

Hyde, Douglas. *I Believed.* New York: G. P. Putnam's, 1946.

Ibarruri, Dolores. "Brave Aragon," *Bulletin of the Political Commissars of the International Brigade,* no. 3, September, 1937.

———. *For the Independence of Spain, for Liberty, for the Republic, Union of All Spaniards: Complete Text of the Report to the Plenary Session of the Central Committee of the Communist Party of Spain, at Madrid on May 23rd, 1938.* Madrid-Barcelona: Communist Party of Spain, 1938.

———. *Ejército popular unido, ejército de la victoria.* Madrid-Barcelona: Ediciones del Partido Comunista de Espana.

———. *Historia del partido comunista de España.* Version abreviada. Warsaw: Ediciones "polonia," 1960.

———. *Speeches and Articles, 1936-1938.* New York: International Publishers, 1938.

———. *El único camino: Memorias de "la Pasionaria."* 3rd edition. Mexico, D. F.: Edicones E.R.A., 1963.

Imerslund, Per. *Viderei passgang: Opplevelser i Mexico og Spania.* Oslo: Kamban [194?].

"In Memory of the Fallen Fighters of the International Brigade in Spain," *The Communist International,* vol. 14, no. 10, October, 1937.

In Spain with the International Brigade. (Collection) London: Burns, Oates and Washburn: 1938.

"The International Brigade," *The Communist International,* vol. 16, no. 3, March 1939. "The International Brigade," *Kommunisticheskii Internatsional* no. 18, December 1936 (translation by X. J. Eudin, Hoover Library, Stanford, California).

International Brigade, Fifteenth. *Le livre de la 15eme brigade internationale: Nos combats contre le fascisme.* Madrid: Ediciones del comisariato de las brigadas internacionales, 1937.

International Brigades. *Canciónes de las brigadas internacionales.* Barcelona: Ediciones del comisariato de las brigadas internacionales, 1938.

———. *Der österreichische Freiwillige.* Madrid: Rivadeneyra, 1938.

———. *Romancero de los voluntarios de la libertad.* Madrid: Ediciones del comisariato de las brigadas internacionales, 1937.

"The International Brigades in Spain," *Revolt,* vol. 3, no. 5, May 1, 1939.

"International Conference in Defense of the Spanish Republic," *International Press Correspondence,* vol. 16, no. 47, October 17, 1936.

International Press Correspondence (London), various issues 1936-38.

Jackson, Gabriel. *The Spanish Republic and the Civil War, 1931-1939.* Princeton, N.J.: Princeton University Press, 1965.

Jellinek, Frank. *The Civil War in Spain.* London: Victor Gollancz, 1938.

Jirku, Gusti. *We Fight Death: The Work of the Medical Services of the International Brigades in Spain*. Madrid: Diana (U.G.T.) n.d.

Kantorowicz, Alfred. *Spanisches Tagebuch*. Berlin: Aufbau Verlag, 1955.

———. *Tschapaiew: das Battalion der 21 Nationen*. Madrid, 1937. East Germany edition: Rudolstadt: F. Mitzlaff, 1953.

Kindelán y Duany, General Alfredo, *Mis cuadernos de Guerra*. Madrid, 1945.

Knoblaugh, H. Edward. *Correspondent in Spain*. London and New York: Sheed and Ward, 1937.

Kolt'sov, Michael. *Ispanski Dnevnik*. Revised edition. Moscow, 1957.

Krivitsky, Walter G. *In Stalin's Secret Service*. New York: Harper, 1939.

———. "Stalin's Hand in Spain." *Saturday Evening Post,* April 15, 1939.

Laird, Megan. "A Diary of Revolution," *Atlantic Monthly,* November 1936.

Lambda. *The Truth About the Barcelona Events*. New York: Workers' Age Publishers, 1937.

Langdon-Davies, John. *Behind the Spanish Barricades*. London: Martin Secker and Warburg Ltd., 1936.

Last, Jef. *The Spanish Tragedy*. Translated from the Dutch by David Hallett. London: G. Routledge and Sons, Ltd., 1939.

League of Nations. *Official Journal*.

———. *Official Journal: Special Supplements 183 and 189.*

Leeds, J. *Let My People Know: The Story of Wilfred ("Mendy") Mendelson*. New York, 1942.

Leone, Francisco. "The International Brigades Yesterday and Today," *The Communist International,* vol. 14, no. 6, June 1937.

Lier, A. H. H. van. *Spanje: Een Land van Tegenstellingen*. Meppel: J. A. Boom en Zoon, 1952.

"The Lincoln Battalion in Pictures," *New Masses,* no. 8, February 14, 1939.

"Lincoln Brigade Number," *New Masses,* No. 8, February 14, 1939.

Lindbaeck, Lise. *Internationella Brigaden*. Stockholm, 1939.

Lizón-Gadea, Adolfo. *Brigadas internacionales en España*. Madrid: Editoria Nacional, 1940.

Lojendio, Luis María de. *Operaciones militares de la guerra de España 1936-1939*. Barcelona: Montaner y Simon, S. A., 1940.

[Longo] Gallo, Luigi. *Un anno di guerra in Spagna*. Paris: Edizioni de Coltura Sociale, 1938.

————. *Brigate internazionali in Spagna, 1936-1939*. Rome: Editori Reuniti, 1956.

López Fernández, Antonio. *Defensa de Madrid*. Mexico, D. F.: A. P. Marquez, 1945.

López, Muñiz. *La batalla de Madrid*. Madrid: F. O. Vincente, 1943.

Loveday, Arthur F. *Spain 1923-1948: Civil War and World War*. Ashcott, Somerset: Boswell Publishing Co. Ltd., 1948.

————. *World War in Spain*. London: John Murray, 1939.

McGovern, John, M. P. *Terror in Spain: How the Communist International Has Destroyed Working Class Unity, Undermined the Fight against Franco, and Suppresses the Social Revolution*. London: Independent Labour Party, n.d.

Machado, Antonio. "El Quinto Regimento del 19 de Julio," *Nuestro ejército*, no. 4, July 1938.

McNeill-Moss, Geoffrey. *The Siege of the Alcazar*. New York: Alfred Knopf, 1937.

Madariaga, Salvador de. *Spain*. New York: Creative Age Press, 1943.

Malraux, André. *L'Espoir*. Paris: Librarie Gallimard, 1937.

Manuilsky, D. *Report of the Delegate of the C.P.S.U. (B) in the Executive Committee of the Communist International to the Eighteenth Congress of the C.P.S.U. (B)*. Delivered March 11, 1939. Moscow, 1939.

Marcel. "The Fifth Column," *Bulletin of the Political Commissars of the International Brigade*, no. 3, September, 1937.

Martin, David. "Jarama: Eleven Years After the Battle," *Spain Today*, vol. 2, no. 7, February, 1948.

Martín Blázquez, José. *I Helped to Build an Army*. Translated by F. Borkenau and Eric Mosbacher. London: Secker and Warburg, 1939.

Martín Retortielo, Cirilo. *Huesca vencedora: Algunos episodios de su heroica defensa*. Huesca: V. Campo, 1938.

Marty, André. "The International Brigade—Twelve Magnificent Months" (Part I), *International Press Correspondence,* vol. 17, no. 45, October 23, 1937.

———. "The International Brigades," *International Press Correspondence,* vol. 18, no. 24, May 17, 1938.

———. "Los voluntarios de la libertad," *Nuestro ejército,* no. 4, July 1938.

"Mathe Zalke," *The Communist International,* vol. 14, no. 9, September 1937.

Matthews, Herbert L. *The Education of a Correspondent.* New York: Harcourt Brace, 1946.

———. *Two Wars and More to Come.* New York: Carrick and Evans, 1938.

Medical Bureau and North American Committee to Aid Spanish Democracy. *Americans in Teruel.* San Francisco, 1938.

———. *From a Hospital in Spain: American Nurses Write.* New York, [1938?].

———. *Report to the Paris Conference on Aid to Republican Spain.* New York (mimeographed), 1938.

Merin, Peter. *Spain Between Death and Birth.* Translated from the German by Charles Fullman. New York: Dodge Publishing Co., 1938.

Morrow, Felix. *Revolution and Counter-Revolution in Spain.* New York: Pioneer Publishers, 1938.

Movimiento libertario español, comité nacional. *Three Years of Struggle in Spain, 1936-1939: The Spanish Revolutionary Union Speaks.* London: The Freedom Press, 1939.

Mundo obrero (newspaper, Madrid and Barcelona).

Muro Negri, D. *La epopeya del Alcazar.* Valladolid: Libreria Santaren, 1937.

Mrozek, Joseph (ed). *Dabrowsrwacy.* Warsaw, 1956.

Negro Committee to Aid Spain. *A Negro Nurse in Republican Spain.* New York, n.d.

Nelson, Steve. *The Volunteers: A Personal Narrative of the Fight Against Fascism in Spain.* New York: Masses and Mainstream, 1953.

Nenni, Pietro. *La guerre d'Espagne*. Paris: François Maspero, 1960.

New Masses (Periodical, New York).

"The New Phase of Struggle for a Democratic, Independent Spain," *The Communist International*, vol. 14, no. 2, February 1937.

Nicoletti, Mario (Guiseppe di Vittorio), "The Victorious Action of the International Legion," *International Press Correspondence*, November 20, 1936.

North, Joseph, *Men in the Ranks: The Story of Twelve Americans in Spain*. Foreword by Ernest Hemingway. New York: Friends of the Abraham Lincoln Brigade, 1939.

Nuestro ejército: Revista militar (Barcelona), various issues, 1938.

"Nuestros voluntarios internacionales: Por qué han venido y por qué se fueron," *Nuestro ejército*, December 1938.

Orlov, Alexander. *The Secret History of Stalin's Crimes*. New York: Random House, 1953.

Orwell, George. *Homage to Catalonia*. London: Secker and Warburg, 1938.

Osorio Tafall, B. F. "Los comisarios en el ejército de la independencia de España," *Nuestro ejército*, no. 4, July 1938.

Pacciardi, Randolfo. *Il battaglione garibaldi: Volontari italiani nella Spagna republicana*. Rome: Edizioni de La Lantera, 1945.

———. Letter to the author, April 17, 1952.

Parker, Dorothy. "Soldiers of the Republic," *Among Friends*, Spring 1938.

Partido comunista de España, comisión nacional de agitacion. *Nuestra gran ejército popular*. (Speech of Carlos Contreras) Barcelona: Ediciones del partido comunista de España, 1937.

Peers, E. Allison. *Catalonia Infelix*. London: Methuen and Co., 1937.

———. *Spain in Eclipse*. London: Methuen and Co., 1943.

Penchienati, Carlo. *Brigate internazionali in Spagna*. Milan: Edizioni "Echi del Secolo," 1950.

Pérez Salas, Jesús. *Guerra en España*. Mexico, D. F., Imprenta Grafos, 1947.

Perla, Mariano. "Los niños y las brigadas internacionales," *Nuestro ejército,* no. 3, June 1938.

Piazzioni, Sandro. *Las tropas flechas negras en la guerra de España, 1937-1939.* Barcelona: Editorial Juventud, 1941.

Pitcairn, Frank. "The International Brigade," *World Review,* January 1937.

———. *Reporter In Spain.* London: Lawrence and Wishart, 1936.

"Plan of Short Courses for Political Delegates," *Bulletin of the Political Commissars of the International Brigade,* October–November 1937.

"The Political Commissar in Spain," *New Masses,* February 14, 21, 1939.

Pollitt, Harry. "In Memory of the British Comrades Who Have Fallen In Spain," *The Communist International,* vol. 14, no. 2, February, 1937.

P.O.U.M. *La política militar del P.O.U.M.* Barcelona: Editorial Marxista, 1937.

Prieto, Carlos [Duff, Charles]. *Spanish Front.* London: Thomas Nelson & Sons, Ltd. 1936.

Prieto, Indalecio. *Como y por qué sali del ministerio de defensa nacional: Intrigas de las Rusos en Espana.* Mexico, D. F.: Impresos y Papeles, S. de R.L., 1940.

The Red Domination in Spain. Madrid: Ministry of Justice, 1946.

Regler, Gustav. *The Great Crusade.* Preface by Ernest Hemingway, translated by Whittaker Chambers and Barrows Mussey. New York: Longmans, Green and Co., 1940.

———. *The Owl of Minerva.* New York: Farrar, Straus and Cudahy, 1959.

Reparez y Tresgallo de Souza, Capitan. *Desde el cuartel General de Miaja al sanctuario de la Virgen de la Cabeza.* Valladolid: Artes Graficas, 1937.

Revolt (incorporating *Spain and the World,* periodical, London).

Riesenfeld, Janet. *Dancer in Madrid.* London and New York: Funk and Wagnalls Co., 1938.

Rodriquez Castillo, Gonzalo. *Communist World Offensive Against Spain.* Madrid: Diplomatic Information Office, 1949.

Rojo, Vicente. *Alerta los pueblos!* Buenos Aires: Aniceto Lopez, 1939.

———. *España heroica.* Buenos Aires: Editorial Americalee, 1942.

Rolfe, Edwin. *The Lincoln Battalion: The Story of the Americans Who Fought in Spain in the International Brigades.* New York: Random House, 1939.

Romilly, Esmond. *Boadilla.* London: H. Hamilton, 1937.

Roux, Georges. *La tragedie Espagnole: La guerre civile D'Espagne.* Paris: Artheme Fayard, 1963.

Rust, William. *Britons in Spain: The History of the British Battalion of the XVth International Brigade,* London: Lawrence and Wishart, 1939.

Sagardia, General. *Del alto Ebro a las fuentes del Llobregat.* Madrid-Barcelona: Editoria Nacional, 1940.

Salter, Cedric. *Try Out in Spain.* New York and London: Harper and Brothers, 1943.

Schwinn, Gretchen. "We Escaped From Madrid," *The National Geographic Magazine,* February 1937.

Sender, Ramon. *Counter Attack in Spain.* Translated from the Spanish by Sir Peters Chalmers-Mitchell. Boston: Houghton-Mifflin Co., 1937.

Sheean, Vincent. *Not Peace but a Sword.* New York: Doubleday, Doran and Co., 1939.

Solidaridad Obrero (newspaper, Madrid).

Sommerfield, John. *Volunteer In Spain.* New York: Alfred Knopf, 1937.

Somoza-Silva, Lazaro. *El General Miaja.* Mexico City: Editorial Tyris. 1944.

Soria, George. "Madrid's Week of Heroism," *International Press Correspondence,* November 21, 1936.

———. *Trotskyism in the Service of Franco: Facts and Documents on the Activities of P.O.U.M.* New York: International Publishers, n.d.

Souchy, Augustin. *The Tragic Week in May.* Barcelona: Oficina de informacion exterior de la C.N.T. y F.A.I., 1937.

Southworth, Herbert. Letter to the author.

Spain (Semi-monthly publication of Spanish Civil War events, New York), various issues, 1937-38.

Spain (Republic), ejército, III Corps. *Brandos, leyes, drecretos, ordenes e instruciones generales de mas frecuente uso.* Granada [1936?].

―――. *Gaceta de la republica: Diario oficial.* Madrid and Valencia.

―――. *The Italian Invasion of Spain (Spanish White Book): Official Documents and Papers Seized from Italian Units in Action at Guadalajara.* Washington, D.C., 1937.

―――, Frente Popular. *The Peoples' Struggle: The Facts and Their Significance.* Madrid, 1936.

Spain (Franco), Office of Spanish Information. *The International Brigades: Foreign Assistants of the Spanish Reds.* Madrid, 1948.

―――, Tribunal supremo, ministerio fiscal. *Datos complementarios para la historia de España: Guerra de Liberacion 1936-1939.* Madrid, 1945.

―――, Tribunal supremo, ministerio fiscal. *La Dominacion rojo en España.* Madrid, 1943.

Spain Today (periodical issued in London by Veterans of the XV Brigade), various issues 1947-51.

Spender, Stephen. *World Within World.* New York: Harcourt, Brace and Co., 1951.

Staborin, J. *Life and Death of an American Hero: The Story of Dave Doran.* New York: New Age Publishers, 1938.

The Story of the Abraham Lincoln Battalion: Written in the Trenches of Spain. New York: Friends of the Abraham Lincoln Battalion, 1938.

Szinda, Gustav. *Die XI Brigade.* Berlin: Verlag des Ministeriums für nationale Verteidigung, 1961.

Taylor, F. J. *The United States and the Spanish Civil War, 1936-1939.* New York: Bookman Associates, 1956.

"Thaelmann's Name All Over the World," *International Press Correspondence,* vol. 16, no. 50, November 7, 1936.

"There's a Valley in Spain," *Spain Today,* vol. 1, no. 8, February 1947.

Thomas, Hugh. *The Spanish Civil War.* New York: Harper and Brothers. 1961.

Tierra y libertad (newspaper, Barcelona).

United States, Department of State. *Documents on German Foreign Policy 1918-1945. Series D, vol. III,* "Germany and the Spanish

Civil War 1936-1939." Washington, D.C.: Government Printing Office, 1950.

―――. *Foreign Relations of the United States*. Washington, D.C.: Government Printing Office, continuing series.

―――. *Peace and War, United States Foreign Policy 1931-1941*. Washington, D.C.: Government Printing Office, 1943.

United States, Subversive Activities Control Board, Docket No. 108-53. Herbert Brownell Jr., Attorney General of the United States, Petitioner, vs. Veterans of the Abraham Lincoln Brigade, Respondent. *Report and Order of the Board*. Washington, D.C., December 1955.

―――. *Order Vacating Registration Order and Dismissing Petition, April, 1966*. Washington, D.C., 1966.

La vanguardia (newspaper, Madrid and Barcelona).

Vittori, A. F. "The War Against Illiteracy," *Bulletin of the Political Commissars of the International Brigade,* no. 3, September 1937.

The Volunteer For Liberty (newspaper, Madrid and Barcelona).

Voros, Sandor. *American Commissar*. Philadelphia and New York: Chilton and Co., 1961.

"Wayfarer," *The International Brigade*. Reprinted from the Weekly Review. Hassocks, Sussex: The Ditchling Press, 1939?

White, D. H., and Hawthorne, J. *From these Honored Dead*. New York: Veterans of the Abraham Lincoln Brigade, 1945.

―――. *Fascist Spain, America's Enemy*. New York: Veterans of the Abraham Lincoln Brigade, 1945.

Wintringham, Thomas H. *English Captain*. London: Faber and Faber, 1939.

"With the International Brigade," *The Nation*, vol. 144, May 8, 1937.

Wolfe, Bertram D. *Civil War In Spain*. New York: Workers Age Publishers, 1937.

Wood, Neal. *Communism and the British Intellectuals*. London: Oxford University Press, 1959.

W.P.A. Teachers' Union Chapter of the Friends of the Abraham Lincoln Brigade. *W.P.A. Teachers in Spain*. New York: Friends of the Abraham Lincoln Brigade, n.d.

Wullschleger, Max (ed). *Schweizer kampfen in Spanien: Erleb-*

nisse der schweizer Freiwilligen in Spanien. Zurich: Verlag der Buchandlung Stauffacter, 1939.

Ypsilon (pseud.). *Pattern For World Revolution.* Chicago and New York: Ziff-Davis, 1947.

Zugazagoitia, Julián. *Historia de la guerra de España.* Buenos Aires: La Vanguardia, 1940.

Index

217